CRAFT BEERS

OF THE
PACIFIC NORTHWEST

A BEER LOVER'S GUIDE to OREGON, WASHINGTON, and BRITISH COLUMBIA

LISA M. MORRISON

Timber Press

PORTLAND | LONDON

To Mark, Mom, and Dad

The author and publisher encourage all readers to visit the
breweries, brewpubs, tasting rooms, and other establishments
mentioned in this book, to sample their beers, but we recommend that those who consume alcoholic beverages travel with
a nondrinking driver. Even pedestrians on pub crawls should
navigate carefully!

Published in 2011 by Timber Press, Inc.

The Haseltine Building
133 S.W. Second Avenue, Suite 450
Portland, Oregon 97204-3527
timberpress.com

2 The Quadrant
135 Salusbury Road
London NW6 6RJ
timberpress.co.uk

Printed in the United States of America
Second printing 2012

A catalog record for this book is also available from the
British Library.

Library of Congress Cataloging-in-Publication Data

Morrison, Lisa M.
  Craft beers of the Pacific Northwest : a beer lover's guide to
Oregon, Washington, and British Columbia / Lisa M. Morrison.
       p. cm.
  Includes bibliographical references and index.
  ISBN 978-1-60469-089-7
  1. Breweries—Northwest, Pacific—Guidebooks. 2. Micro-
breweries—Northwest, Pacific—Guidebooks. 3. Northwest,
Pacific—Guidebooks. I. Title.
  TP577.M674 2011
  641.2'309795—dc22
                          2010032648

CONTENTS

INTRODUCTION

From the end of Prohibition until about three decades ago, beer in America meant only one thing: a fizzy, pale, nearly flavorless liquid that was best served ice-cold. It was the cheap white bread of the wider beer world, a mass-produced product made of inferior filler ingredients, peddled by its makers for the sole purpose of making as much money as possible.

Then came a shift—a tiny tremor in northern California, where a small, short-lived brewery got the whole thing rolling. Oregon and Washington soon followed suit, and the shakeup spread north to British Columbia. Throughout the Pacific Northwest, a handful of pioneers began exploring ways to make beer with flavor, brewed from local ingredients, as it once was made. They wanted to make beer with integrity, and people wanted to drink it.

These craft beer pioneers overcame many obstacles. They scrounged for ingredients. They convinced politicians to change laws so they could make and sell their beer. They welded and jury-rigged old dairy equipment for use in their tiny breweries. And, after all that, they still faced their toughest challenge yet: they needed to persuade beer drinkers, familiar with only the mass-produced beers of the day, to sample their odd-looking, cloudy beers that were made in small batches just down the street. Fortunately, Northwesterners are not only pioneering but also adventurous people. "Microbrew," as it was called back in the day, caught on quickly, and the Northwest became the cradle of the craft beer movement that is now flourishing and spreading across the United States, Canada, and the world.

Much like *terroir* in wine, these new craft beers possess defining characteristics. But instead of being shaped by the soil's condition or mineral content, craft beer's *terroir* is influenced by the personalities of the brewers, the surrounding communities, and the particular culture that envelops each brewery. I have been writing about beer for more than a dozen years, and I still can't quite put my finger on it—that enigmatic quality that gives craft beer a slightly different flavor in the Pacific Northwest. It could be that artisan brewers have been making beer in this region for upwards of 30 years. Perhaps it is the quality and freshness of the ingredients—the Northwest is the heart of the largest hops-growing area on the continent. Or maybe those old beer ads were right after all. Maybe it *is* the water.

I prefer to believe that it's the people—the Northwest brewers and the beer fans who, through their passions, continue to put their own indelible mark on craft beer.

ACKNOWLEDGMENTS

I'm blessed to have many of these wonderful people to thank for their contributions to this book.

First and foremost, my heart and my heartfelt thanks go to Mark Campbell, my wonderful and patient husband, who makes me laugh every day. Mark has been with me either in person or in supportive spirit every day throughout the research and writing of this book. Whether it was driving us across western British Columbia with our dog, Yeti, so I could concentrate on research, calling to check in each night when I was on the road alone, or cooking dinner so I could squeeze in some more writing time, those generous gestures and your companionship meant so much.

A lifetime of gratitude to Joe and Nancy Morrison, my parents, who always told me I could do anything I wanted to do (although I am convinced "beer writer" never crossed your minds).

It is a great pleasure to express my thanks to the following friends: Susan and Dan Bartlett, my travel mates, who assisted more than they will ever know on beer research trips; Susan Benson, who smilingly took on the task of looking up contact information for the listings in this book; John Norton, who stepped in and made phone calls so I could focus on writing at a crucial time; John Foyston, who first suggested I write this book; and Eric and Valerie Bressman, who were always there to lend an ear, ride "shotgun" on a photo-taking mission to Seattle, or help out with a pub crawl.

Many thanks to Rick Green, of the Campaign for Real Ale in Vancouver, B.C., for being just an e-mail away to answer a question or confirm a fact, and to Don Scheidt, Mike Besser, Tiffany Hereth Adamowski, and Jake Swanke, who helped me make heads *and* tails out of the Seattle beer scene.

Finally, sincere thanks and deep gratitude to all the brewers, brewery and pub owners, servers, distributors, promoters, fellow beer writers, and beer enthusiasts who passionately contribute to the exceptional beer culture—this beer community—that we are so fortunate to enjoy in the Pacific Northwest.

ABOUT THIS BOOK

The topography of craft beer is ever-changing here in the Pacific Northwest, just like it is all over the world. That's what makes it so intriguing and exciting. So, instead of thinking of this book as the quintessential fixed-in-stone roadmap to craft beer in the Pacific Northwest, think of it as more of a compass. The people you will meet and the places you will visit in the pages of this book have all contributed to the region's vibrant craft beer culture. Nothing can change that. The roots of craft beer have already grown deep here; the past is so rich and the future so compelling that you will want to explore the present Northwest beer community all on your own. A good number of websites, including my own—-beergoddess.com—-help you keep track of the latest news at (and most current information concerning) the taps and the breweries.

The book opens with a primer, Beer 101—how beer is made, how beer is styled, and "beer talk," a glossary of some of the more unusual beer terms you'll encounter in these pages. The three main chapters offer an in-depth look at Oregon, Washington, and British Columbia, in turn. Much like a map is laid out, allowing you to narrow in on the specific area you are looking for, within each of these, the state or province and especially the larger cities are divided into regions or neighborhoods. You can thumb through the pages to find an exact location, or let your mind take you on a virtual trip through this rich land of craft beers.

Throughout, you will find a bit of history, some fun facts about beer, or a profile of one of the Northwest's craft beer pioneers. And every once in a while, you will discover a pub crawl that I've designed for a specific location. The pub crawls are intended for walking; there is never a stretch between destinations that is much more than a mile long—just long enough to work up a bit of a thirst. Again, feel free to use these pub crawls not so much as a roadmap but as a compass to guide you through your own craft beer explorations, and be sure to always use caution when you are a pedestrian. As if it needs saying: don't drink and drive! Use public transportation when possible. If you are exploring by car, always plan on having a designated nondrinking companion in your party.

Within the three main chapters, you will find details for all the breweries listed in the book's margins for quick reference. After all, without Northwest breweries and Northwest beer, we wouldn't be able to enjoy our rich Northwest beer culture. Then, at the end of the book, you will find a city guide for each of the three regions, with listings for the non-brewing establishments mentioned in these chapters, plus some other fine, craft beer–focused locations intended to help you chart your own beer expeditions, should you be "thirsty for more." In all these listings, I designate what type of establishment it is, so you know what to expect:

A brewery is a production facility that normally is not open to the public. Please call ahead of time to arrange an appointment with these breweries.

 A brewery/tasting room is a production brewery with posted public hours and possibly even a space for tasting the beers.

 A brewpub is a brewery that also is in the business of serving food along with its beers.

A pub is an establishment that offers a number of different taps (and possibly bottled beers) featuring different beer styles from a variety of breweries. For the purposes of this book, this term is synonymous with alehouses, tap rooms, and tap houses.

Any restaurant mentioned, especially as a stop in a pub crawl, can be expected to have a good craft beer selection (or be very close to an establishment that does!).

Also included is a separate listing of bottle shops—the best of the places that sell a wide selection of bottled beers. Some might even be pubs, allowing you to drink the beers onsite.

As always, please enjoy craft beer in a responsible manner, and respect its delightful abilities to enhance some of the most precious pleasures on earth, those of friendship, delicious food and drink, good cheer, and the fine art of conversation. Cheers!

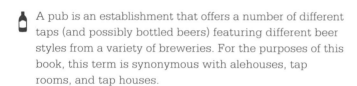

SEVEN "DON'T MISS" BOTTLE SHOPS

1. Belmont Station & Biercafé, Portland, Ore.
2. Bier Stein, Eugene, Ore.
3. Bottleworks, Seattle, Wash.
4. Brewery Creek Cold Beer & Wine, Vancouver, B.C.
5. By the Bottle, Vancouver, Wash.
6. John's Market, Portland, Ore.
7. 99 Bottles, Federal Way, Wash.

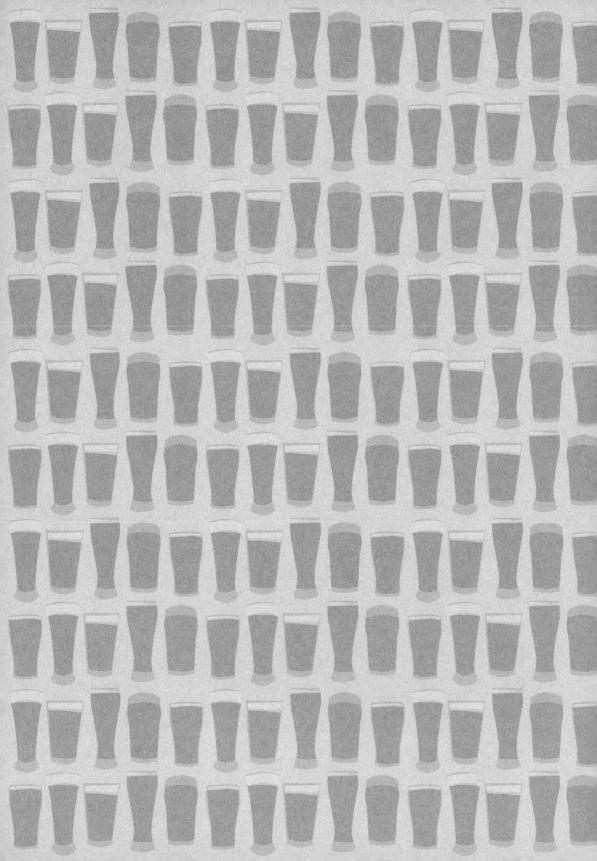

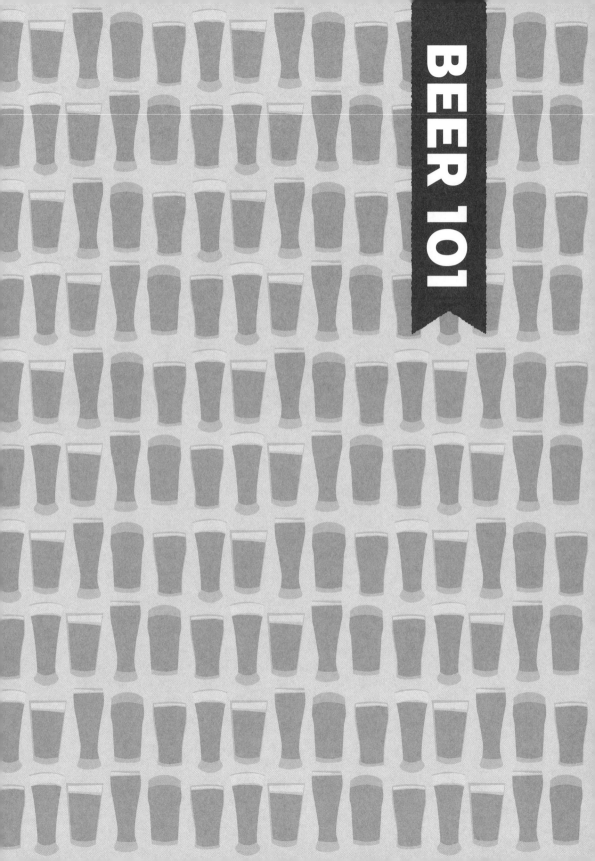

BEER 101

Four basic ingredients go into making beer, with seemingly endless results.

BEER 101

Beer is one of the oldest fermented beverages, dating back to the ancient Sumerians of Mesopotamia, who worshipped the goddess Ninkasi. This high priestess was the ultimate head brewer, in charge of all things related to beer and beer-making. What is possibly the oldest beer recipe on record, a hymn to Ninkasi, details how the Sumerians made their magic elixir (when the filtered beer was poured out in the final stanzas, it was "like the onrush of Tigris and Euphrates"). The recipe was passed from generation to generation in song and with blessings for the beer and for Ninkasi.

Brewing has changed a lot since, but the basic ingredients really haven't (although hops, the most recent addition, didn't come significantly into play until the 15th century). Made up of only four ingredients—grains, water, hops, and yeast—beer is astoundingly complex in its simplicity. A skilled brewer can take those four ingredients and create a myriad of beers that are different in color, aroma, flavor, and even texture.

Brewers in the Pacific Northwest are particularly blessed. They have easy access to an abundance of the best and freshest beer ingredients in the world, making Northwest beer a truly local product. The water sources Northwest brewers use are both plentiful and pristine. The majority of the hops grown in the United

States are nurtured and harvested on Northwest farms. While most malt is still shipped from elsewhere, an increasing number of brewers are using at least some grain that is grown or malted in the region. And Northwest brewers can work closely—often face-to-face—with the fermentation experts at Wyeast Laboratories in Odell, Ore., one of the world's predominant purveyors and cultivators of yeast strains since 1986.

MAKING BEER

Whether it's a homebrewed India pale ale created five gallons at a time or a commercial, macrobrewed lager made in a batch more than 4,000 times that size, the basics of making beer are the same. Beer is produced by steeping a starch source (grain) in water to create a liquid that contains sugars. The sugars provide food for another key ingredient, yeast, which creates the fermentation by eating the sugars in the liquid and converting it to alcohol. Before fermentation—and sometimes during and after—hops are added to supply certain qualities, including flavor and aroma.

Let's take a look at the four ingredients to see how each contributes to that final tasty beer.

WATER. Beer is more than 90 percent water. The different chemical and mineral components of that water can influence the flavor of the beer, to the extent that certain beer styles can be duplicated only by altering the chemical and mineral content of locally available water. For instance, English pale ales traditionally use water that is "hard," like the water in Burton-upon-Trent, where the style originated. A brewer using another water source might need to add minerals so the water mimics that hardness to replicate the beer style. Fortunately, the water sources in the Pacific Northwest are generally very "soft," with little chemical or mineral influence, which makes for a clean slate in creating different beer styles.

MALT AND OTHER GRAINS. Grains create the palette that brewers draw from to design each beer, helping them achieve the colors, aromas, flavors, and textures they want in each brew. Grains are the multi-taskers of the beer world. They impart carbs (sugars) into the water in which they are steeped, creating a liquid called "wort"; those sugars become food for the yeast that ferments the wort, creating alcohol and turning that wort into beer.

Barley is the predominant grain in beer, although wheat, oats, sorghum, and other grains can be used, often in conjunction with barley. Malted barley (or malt for short) is simply barley that has undergone the malting process, in which grains are germinated and put into a kiln for drying. Depending on the temperature and

(Above) Different grains create the brewer's palette. (Below) Hops in an Oregon field are ready for harvest.

the amount of time spent in the kiln, the grains can be lightly toasted or as darkly roasted as espresso coffee beans. That difference can impart varying flavors as well as colors in the beer. Think of it like a piece of toasted bread: a lighter toast on the bread gives you a flavor that is different from a darker one. It's the same with barley. Grains that are pale in color make for beers that are lighter in color as well as contributing flavors like bread dough, biscuit, and toast. Medium-toasted grains impart a darker color and flavors like caramel and toffee. Brown to black-colored grains can be used to darken a beer's color and will introduce chocolate, coffee, and, at the farthest end of the spectrum, even a slight yet pleasant burnt note.

When other grains are used, the resulting beer will have yet another suite of flavors, color, and "mouthfeel." The oatmeal used in an oatmeal stout, for instance, gives the beer a smooth texture and sweetness in flavor; wheat can give beer a creamy mouthfeel and a grainy quality in both aroma and flavor. A brewer will typically use a variety of different malts and grains to achieve the color, flavor, aroma, and mouthfeel desired in a beer. That list of grains is referred to as the beer's grain bill, or grist.

HOPS. These small, green, cone-shaped flowers (or strobiles, to be botanically precise) are the spice of beer. Hops develop on tall, fast-climbing bines, not vines, sometimes growing as much as a foot a day. When they are ready for harvest, the flowers are separated from the bines and dried to preserve them for use during the entire year until the next harvest. Depending on the variety, hops can be used to balance out sweetness, create a desired bitterness, and lend certain aromas in a beer. In the past, especially, hops were also used to prevent beer from spoiling; their antibacterial properties act as a natural preservative.

There is a rich history of hop-growing in the Pacific Northwest, from the Frasier Valley in British Columbia to the Willamette Valley in Oregon. In the past, entire families would migrate to the hop fields in these rural areas to help hand-pick the hops off the scratchy, prickly bines—a process that could often take weeks. Worldwide, only Germany exceeds Washington and Oregon in hop production.

Oregon State University is one of the leading international researchers in cultivating new hop varieties; the Corvallis-based university's agriculture department has a long history of working with Oregon hop farmers, and some of the region's hop growers even have a plot or two of land designated for test hops to help OSU learn how the new hop strains perform. In 2010, the College of Agricultural Sciences at OSU created an aroma hop breeding program, designed to work closely with existing hop research at OSU. While bittering hops are primarily used by large, industrial brewers to provide a balance to the sweetness of the malt, the aroma hops that OSU is studying are prized by craft brewers for the different flavor and aroma nuances that they impart in beer. The Pacific Northwest is known for its highly hopped beers, and the proximity of many breweries to the hop yards helps boost the enthusiasm for the hoppy beers that emanate from the region. Many Northwest brewers celebrate the annual hop harvest in late summer by brewing fresh-hop, sometimes called wet-hop, beers. The brewers will start the brewing process, letting the malt steep in the wort while they hurry to the hop yards for freshly picked hops. With trucks loaded, the brewers make a mad dash back to their breweries, and the hops are popped into the wort, sometimes within an hour or two of being plucked off the bines.

WHAT IS "DRY-HOPPING"?

Northwest brewers are famous for dry-hopping beer. But what is dry-hopping?

Typically, hops are added to the brewing liquor during the brewing process. These hop additions can be made several times during the process; each time adds a different nuance, as the boiling, malty liquid dissolves the lupulin (a sticky substance in hops that contains volatile oils which, in turn, flavor the beer).

In dry-hopping, hops are added to a beer *after the boil.* Because some of those oils aren't boiled away in the brew kettle, dry-hopping increases hop flavor and aroma in the beer. Dry-hopping a beer is like adding an herb shortly before serving versus cooking with it. Both methods impart flavor, but the former yields a flavor that is more pronounced.

YEAST. Tiny but mighty, these microscopic organisms shoulder a lot of responsibility. After all, it is yeast that creates fermentation by consuming the sugar in the wort and leaving behind alcohol. The other byproduct from hard-working yeast is carbonation: yeast gives beer its effervescence. That's pretty heady stuff in itself, but yeast brings a lot more than that to the beer table. It is the strain of yeast that determines whether a beer is an ale or a lager, the two main families of beer.

Yeast determines whether a beer is an ale or a lager.

Caldera Kettle Series ~ A Limited Small Batch Seasonal Release
Caldera Brewing Company • Ashland Oregon

Ale yeasts, or top-fermenting yeasts, like to work in warm temperatures and typically form a layer of foam on the surface of the beer while they are creating fermentation. They also tend to work quickly; ales are usually ready to drink about three weeks after fermentation begins. Lager yeasts do their job more slowly, in cooler temperatures. They

This Belgian-style wheat ale will taste different from a German one, partly because of the yeast that was used.

are referred to as bottom-fermenting because they collect at the bottom of the vessel during fermentation. It's not uncommon for lagers to be stored in a cool fermenter for more than a month while the yeasts do their thing, and it's no coincidence that the word *lager* means "storage" in German.

Some yeasts contribute hardly any flavor to beer at all, but others are distinctive. For example, a German hefeweizen will exhibit banana, clove, and other spicy notes because of the traditional German yeast that is used. In general, ale yeasts tend to impart more diverse flavors, while lager yeasts create a smoother, rounder finish in the beer.

So, just based on these four ingredients, consider the number of decisions that might go into brewing a beer:

- Should the water be altered?
- Which types of grains and how much of each should be used to obtain the desired level of sugars in the wort for both alcohol content and mouthfeel? What grains need to be added to create the desired flavors and color?
- To achieve the desired bitterness, balance, and aromas, which hops should be used and in what quantity? When should they be added?
- Which yeast strain should be used, lager or ale? What other characteristics should the yeast contribute?

And that's just the beginning. There's a lot of "think" that goes into that drink. Beer is part science, part art, and wholly a thing of beauty.

BEER STYLES

So, we know now that beer's family tree starts with either lager or ale yeast. But those are pretty broad descriptions. When someone asks what beer you want, have you ever simply replied "an ale"? Probably not. You order a specific type of beer, and when you do, you expect that beer to have certain properties—hoppiness in an IPA, for example, or a spicy effervescence in a hefeweizen. If that hefeweizen you ordered arrives black in color and tasting like chocolate and coffee, you probably know you got the wrong beer. But *how* do you know that?

Beer styles to the rescue! The Beer Judge Certification Program has been keeping tabs on the world's great beer styles since 1985, helping beer lovers, judges, brewers, bartenders, and others talk to each other about beer by providing a common language and a standardized set of descriptions, so we can all be on the proverbial same page (or, at least, the same chapter!). So, when that hefeweizen you ordered comes out looking more like an imperial stout, you have some pretty solid reasons for thinking it's not what you ordered.

Sticking with our hefeweizen example, let's examine the five main elements that make up a beer style—appearance, aroma, flavor, mouthfeel, and strength.

APPEARANCE. This black-colored beer that was just set in front of you looks nothing like a hefeweizen, which—style dictates—should range in color from pale straw to a deep gold. Now, in this case, the discrepancy in color is obvious, but in other cases, it's not that easy. Color can be subjective.

Enter the Standard Reference Method, or SRM, a scale that is used to determine color ranges in beer. Judges use it to determine if a beer's color is "within style," something that could make or break a potential award-

Knowing basic beer styles helps you determine what flavors you like.

B BREWING Co · · R&B BREWING C

R&B

ICEHOLES

· CELEBRATION LAGER ·

A traditional European style lager

650 ml Beer Bière 5.0% alc./vol.

winner. Brewers (especially competitive ones!) use the SRM to determine which grains will help them achieve the desired color for a specific beer style. The rest of us might just want to stick to the eyeball technique: look at the beer that's been put in front of you and determine if its color is similar to what you expected when you ordered it. You would be surprised how many times at festivals and even some pubs, a beer line will get crossed and the beer being poured isn't what the tap says it is.

Appearance, though, is more than just color. You can tell a lot about a beer by its clarity, how lively it is in the glass, how much head it has, and even what the bubbles look like—are they large and quick-lived or are they tight, making an almost meringue consistency? It pays to pay attention to what your beer looks like. I've actually been able to guess what beer people are drinking just by noticing its appearance. It's a great bar trick.

AROMA. The aroma is formed from the malt, the amount of alcohol, the type of hops, the yeast strain, and even the water and the brewing process itself. If we go back to our "black" hefeweizen, style notes tell us that a German hefeweizen should have some strong spicy and fruity aromas, such as clove and banana. The aromas from this black-colored beer are of coffee and dark chocolate, not bananas. Aroma makes up quite a bit of what you taste, so if you smell these aromas, you are probably going to taste them, too.

FLAVOR. The components that affect aroma also contribute to a beer's flavor, including the types and amounts of malt used, the yeast, the alcohol level, the water, and the hops—what type, how

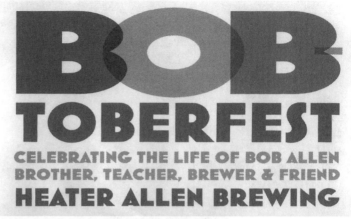

BOB TOBERFEST

CELEBRATING THE LIFE OF BOB ALLEN
BROTHER, TEACHER, BREWER & FRIEND
HEATER ALLEN BREWING

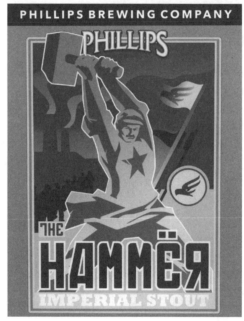

much, and when and how the hops were added to the beer. Bitterness from hops is measured with the International Bittering Units scale. Generally, the higher the IBU number, the more bitterness will be perceived when you drink the beer. But bitterness is less noticeable in beers that use a lot of malt. A higher IBU is needed in these heavier beers to balance the flavor. In the case of the mystery black beer that we have in front of us, it might have a higher IBU value, even though it might not taste as hoppy as another beer.

MOUTHFEEL. Another clue to a beer's style is "mouthfeel," or, not surprisingly, how the beer actually feels in your mouth. The texture can be effervescent, like that of a sparkling wine, or it might be nearly free of carbonation, giving it a velvety smoothness, with varying levels in-between. There is also the heaviness of the beer; one beer might feel rich and thick in the mouth, while another could have a thin consistency. The finish of a beer can be considered part of the flavor or the mouthfeel. Some beers have a lingering flavor while others just drop off. Like wine, a beer can finish sweet or dry. Our mystery black beer is rich, velvety smooth and heavy in the mouth, with a lingering finish of coffee and chocolate. A hefeweizen should never be heavy, but might feel a bit creamy and spritzy. Another clue it's not the right beer!

STRENGTH. This is the general term for the amount of alcohol in the beer. It can either be perceived by how it affects you, or it might be presented on the beer label or listing, usually expressed as alcohol by volume, or ABV.

An imperial stout, by style, is a high-alcohol beer. Hefeweizens are not. This mystery beer has not met a single style guideline for a hefeweizen. Time to send it back! Or give it to me. I love a good imperial stout.

BEER TALK: A GLOSSARY

Beer definitely speaks its own language. Fortunately, you don't have to know the language to love the beer, but it does help to pick up a few terms so you can speak intelligently with other beer people. Here are some terms and their definitions as used in this book and/or in the region.

ABBEY ALE: a beer brewed in the tradition of Trappist monks.

ABV: alcohol by volume.

ALE: one of the two main families of beers, made with top-fermenting yeast.

ALEHOUSE: an establishment that offers a wide variety of beers on draft and/or in the bottle, but doesn't have a brewery onsite.

BARLEY WINE: a strong beer style with an ABV between 8 and 14 percent, rivaling fruit wine. Barley wines often age as well as fruit wines.

BEER ENGINE: also known as a hand pump, this airtight device is used to siphon beer from a cask into a glass without extra carbon dioxide (CO_2). Pulling down on the handle raises a piston which draws the beer.

BREWERIANA: a collection of items that relate to beer and brewing, including cans, glasses, serving trays, and photos.

CAMRA: Campaign for Real Ale, a British-based organization that is, by its own definition, "an independent, voluntary, consumer organization which campaigns for real ale, real pubs and consumer rights." There is a strong CAMRA chapter in British Columbia.

CASK, CASK-CONDITIONED ALE: unfiltered and unpasteurized beer that is conditioned and served from a cask without adding any extra gas to force it out of the cask. Sometimes referred to as "real ale."

CRAFT BEER: beer that is, according the Brewers Association definition, "small, independent, and traditional." Sometimes referred to as "artisan beer."

DRY-HOPPED: a technique in which, hops are added to beer after it has fermented, contributing to the flavor and aroma.

DUBBEL: a Belgian or Belgian-style ale that is brewed in the Dubbel (or Double) style.

ESB: extra special bitter, a beer with English roots. The name was originally used for English pale ales.

IBU: International Bittering Units, a value that can provide a rough estimate of how bitter a beer might be. The higher the number, the more bitter the beer.

IPA: India pale ale, an English pale ale that was made higher in alcohol and with more hops to preserve the beer as it made its way on a boat to colonizing British troops in India. The Pacific Northwest has adopted the IPA as its craft beer style of choice, upping the hop levels significantly compared to the British versions.

LAGER: one of the two main families of beers, made with bottom-fermenting yeast.

LAMBIC: a beer style originating in Belgium that is fermented with wild yeast instead of carefully cultivated brewer's yeast strains, lending dry, vinous, slightly sour flavors.

LOCAL: the pub or alehouse that one frequents, as in, "The Horse Brass is Don's local. I see him there all the time."

MOUTHFEEL: the texture of the beer in your mouth; literally how it feels in the mouth.

NITRO: nitrogen; sometimes used under high pressure (instead of the more common CO_2) when dispensing dry Irish stouts and other creamy beers because it helps to form a rich, thick head and makes the beer feel smoother in the mouth.

NUT BROWN ALE: a Northern English brown-style ale made from malts that impart pleasant nutty flavors.

ROTATING TAP: a tap head that isn't always designated for the same beer. Many pubs will feature at least a few rotating taps because patrons appreciate variety.

TAP HOUSE: another word for an alehouse.

TAP LIST: the menu of beers available on draft at an establishment.

TAPROOM: a place that is usually connected to a brewery where people can gather to sample the beers or even buy full glasses of the beers, without its being a full-fledged brewpub. Some establishments (and this book) use the term interchangeably with pub, tap house, and alehouse.

TASTER TRAY: a collection of beers in small portions so a customer can sample different selections. Also called a sample tray or sampler tray.

TRIPEL: a Belgian or Belgian-style ale that is brewed in the Tripel (sometimes Triple or Trippel) style.

WIT: a Belgian-style wheat beer that is very different from German or American wheat beers. Wits are typically fruitier, often with hints of lemon or orange peel. The use of coriander and other spices is very common in wits.

WORT: in the brewing process, the liquid that is produced from steeping grains and adding hops before yeast is added.

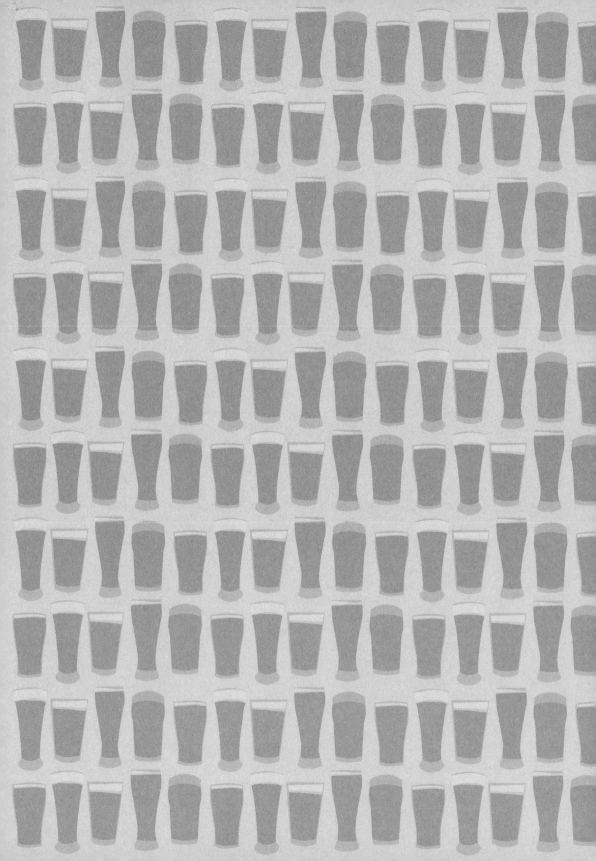

OREGON

OREGON

British beer writer Pete Brown called Oregon the heart and soul of craft beer, and indeed Oregon's craft brewers are esteemed around the world for quality and innovation. The earliest brewers have been at work for decades, and their numbers increase every day. According to the Oregon Brewers Guild, more than 80 brewing companies call Oregon home—operating more than 100 brewing facilities across the state, creating new beer styles, winning international awards, and keeping Oregon on the map as one

Oregon is home to more than 80 breweries.

of the world's best places for brewing and enjoying artisan beer. But it's not just the breweries that make Oregon so unique; it's the beer fans as well. Oregonians drink up nearly 40 percent of all the draft beer produced in the state, and because there are no large, industrial breweries in Oregon, that is all craft beer, baby.

PORTLAND METRO

Portland is the cradle of the modern-day brewpub, and that important distinction is evident citywide, with brewpubs scattered across the metro area. With more than 35 brewing facilities currently (and growing by at least a couple every year), Portland is home to more breweries than any other city in the world. It's a rare day that something beer-related isn't happening here, be it a launch of a new brew, a beer dinner, or a "Meet the Brewer" event in which fans flock to talk face-to-face with a craft brewer from around the globe or around the corner and taste his or her wares. Portland is home to the Oregon Brewers Festival, one of the largest and oldest beer festivals in the country, which is kicked off each year with an official parade of brewers and beer fans marching through downtown. A handful of other large beer festivals are spaced judiciously throughout the calendar, including the Spring Beer & Wine Fest, always the Friday and Saturday of Easter

BEST FESTS: OREGON

Fresh Hop Tastivals
several locations in October
oregonbeer.org

Holiday Ale Festival
Portland, holidayale.com

North American Organic Brewers Festival
Portland, naobf.org

Oregon Brewers Festival
Portland, oregonbrewfest.com

Portland International Beer Festival
Portland, seattlebeerfest.com

Sasquatch Brew Fest
Eugene, northwestlegendsfoundation.org

Spring Beer & Wine Fest
Portland, springbeerfest.com

weekend, and the Holiday Ale Festival, which takes place the first weekend in December, making it easy to celebrate craft beer in Portland year-round.

As impressive as all that is, it's not the big events that shape Portland's beer culture; it's the small, day-to-day stuff. Walk in any gas station convenience store, and I guarantee you will find several shelves in the cooler devoted to craft beer. Some convenience stores even hang up signs touting their selection of hundreds of craft beer inside. Grocery stores stock row upon row of craft beer—enough to make out-of-town visitors drop to their knees in awe. Brewpubs dot the entire landscape in Portland, but you also can order a local craft beer at just about any dive bar, college hangout, neighborhood pub, or mom-and-pop tavern, and just as easily find another one at the fanciest restaurants in town. No wonder Portland is called Beervana!

Geographically, Portland is bisected vertically by the Willamette River, into the east and west sides, and horizontally by Burnside Street, which creates the north and south halves of the city. The cross hairs yield quadrants: Northeast, Northwest, Southeast, and Southwest. But Portlanders like to "keep Portland weird" (it's the city's unofficial motto), so don't be surprised that there's a "fifth quadrant," North Portland. Let's take this nomenclature and run with it for this segment of the book; it's an easy way to navigate through the beer topography that makes up Beervana.

BIRTH OF THE BREWPUB

The Barley Mill, the beginning of the McMenamins empire.

You can't go too far in Portland without finding yourself in front of brewpub. Most are family-friendly, offering craft sodas, kid menus, toys, and coloring books alongside a wide selection of food and craft beer. It was not always this way. The Rose City has a shady past, including a 19th-century Shanghaiing trade that continued well into the 20th century. With such notorious beginnings, it's hard to reconcile Portland's first tavern scenes with today's bright, warm, and welcoming public houses. This is how it happened.

In 1974, a young Oregon State University graduate named Mike McMenamin teamed up with some college buddies and opened Produce Row, the first modern-style tap house in Oregon. McMenamin wanted Produce Row to mirror what he saw when he traveled Europe after graduation: neighborhood pubs and cafés that were open to all ages. McMenamin also had developed a taste for European beer, and discovered that distributors were able to supply him with a growing variety of imports. Produce Row, named for the stretch along Portland's inner eastside where local vegetables and fruit were processed and sold, became a beer mecca. And despite changing hands several times, ProRow, as the locals call it, carries on the legacy.

A few years later, McMenamin officially partnered with his younger brother, Brian. Because the two had been working together for years, Mike McMenamin admits he has a hard time recalling exactly which establishment should be considered the first "official" McMenamins pub, but the company's website taps the Barley Mill, on SE Hawthorne, for the honor.

Soon after the brothers opened the Barley Mill, Oregon law changed to allow breweries to sell beer on-premises, and the McMenamins Hillsdale Brewery & Public House in southwest Portland became the first brewpub in the state. For the McMenamins, these ventures were the first pieces of an eclectic empire that continues to flourish. For Portland, and the rest of the country, they were the prototypes for the modern brewpub, a place where people gather to enjoy good beer and the warmth of community in its fullest sense.

Hillsdale Brewery & Public House
1505 SW Sunset Blvd., Portland, 503-246-3938, mcmenamins.com

NORTH PORTLAND

This "Fifth Quadrant" has undergone a renaissance of sorts over the past several years; it is now one of the most vibrant communities in Portland, as the number of great beer places within its borders attests.

A beer excursion in Portland isn't complete without stopping at the Widmer Gasthaus Pub. Brothers Kurt and Rob Widmer are true U.S. beer pioneers; in the dark days, they had to drag kegs of their beer from bar to bar in Portland and beyond, giving away free samples to encourage folks to buy their "odd-looking" beer. The Widmers are also credited with creating the American-style hefeweizen, now their flagship beer and copied across the country. Interestingly, it was not the ubiquitous hefeweizen that the Widmers first tried to sell around Portland more than two decades ago, when they were just firing up their brew kettles. That distinction goes to their altbier, and to this day, the alt is greeted with much fanfare by adoring beer lovers every time a batch is released at the Gasthaus.

Sure, you can get Widmer beers in most states, but the Gasthaus is where all the special brews are released. Ask which Collaborator beers are on draft when you go. Collaborator is a joint project between Widmer and the Oregon Brew Crew homebrew

**WIDMER
GASTHAUS PUB**
955 N. Russell St.
Portland, 503-281-3333
widmer.com

club, in which winners of an annual club-only competition get to brew their recipe on Widmer's small pilot system. The beers are on tap at the Gasthaus and distributed at other beer bars in the area, with proceeds from sales earmarked for a scholarship in fermentation sciences at Oregon State University. The project, among the first of its kind in the country, is a way for the Widmers to give back to the homebrewing community.

As large as Widmer Brothers Brewing is,

(Above) Kurt and Rob Widmer were among Portland's, and the nation's, beer pioneers. (Below) Judges determine which homebrews "go pro" in Collaborator competitions.

**UPRIGHT
BREWING CO.**

240 N. Broadway #2
Portland, 503-735-5337
uprightbrewing.com

Upright Brewing Co. is as small. Located in the Leftbank Project Building, in the shadow of the Rose Quarter Arena, Upright is a production brewery with a small, casual tasting room right inside. Like the Widmer brothers did more than 20 years before, owner-brewermaster Alex Ganum is breaking all the moulds with his French-Belgian inspired, open-fermented beers. The tasting room features eight or nine taps. Four are reserved for Upright's base beers, simply named Four, Five, Six, and Seven, for their starting gravity, or the percentage of sugar content in the wort before fermentation. Four is a light and refreshing beer with a hint of sourness; Five is a farmhouse ale (a style to which Ganum is clearly devoted) that is benefitted by a heavy hand with hops; Six is a rye beer, a bit more complex with a tart, dry finish; and Seven is a spicy-fruity beer with a lively lingering hop finish. The offerings on the other taps rotate according to Ganum's experimentations.

Upright has open hours on Fridays, Saturdays, and Sundays, as well as being open for a few hours before Portland Trailblazer's evening home games. Please be sure to contact Upright ahead of time if you want to visit. As a side note, the name Upright is homage to the building's past: in a former life, it was home to a jazz club, where upright basses were employed.

Saraveza Bottle Shop & Pasty Tavern is a top-notch taproom and bottle shop. Owner Sarah Pederson, a transplanted Wisconsinite, has covered every wall with beer paraphernalia, most of which she acquired in her home state. The tabletops are even swathed in bottle caps from different breweries across the country. Emphasizing American craft and Belgian beers, Saraveza offers a selection of unusual, new, and hard-to-find beers on ten rotating taps, plus another 200 or so bottled beers in completely refurbished old-fashioned coolers. Have fun perusing them. Sara-

Unlike their seasonals, like the Gose, Upright's year-round beers are simply named with numbers

veza is small, but what it lacks in space it makes up for in beery enthusiasm.

The 5th Quadrant is Lompoc Brewery's flagship location, a bit more upscale in both atmosphere and menu items than the other, more casual Lompoc locations. It is by far Lompoc's largest space, home to Lompoc's main brewery and its barrel-aging project, which is the theme in the adjacent Side Bar tasting room. Opened in 2009, the Side Bar offers a cozy fireplace, several beers on tap, and some specialty beers in bottles; they'll often be pouring crazy stuff from those barrels that you can't get at the other locations. Hours are limited, so check ahead.

At either the 5th Quadrant or the Side Bar, you can choose from Lompoc's lineup of base beers, including the bracingly beautiful C-Note Imperial Pale Ale, made with all the classic "C" hops (Cascade, Centennial, Cluster, Chinook, and Crystal) and the smoky, toffee-like LSD, or Lompoc Strong Draft; this last brew is bottled as Lompoc Special Draft: the federal government wouldn't allow Lompoc to have the word "strong" on the label.

5TH QUADRANT & SIDE BAR
3901 N. Williams Ave.
Portland, 503-288-3996
newoldlompoc.com

DON'T MISS

- Altbier, Kurt and Rob Widmer's first professionally brewed beer, and still one of their best, at the Gasthaus.

- Upright Brewing's envelope-pushing, open-fermentation beers.

- Getting into the Wisco vibe with world-class beers and breweriana at Saraveza.

- Swallowing some LSD (Lompoc Strong Draft) at the 5th Quadrant, then slipping over to the Side Bar for some experimental barrel-beer tasting.

NORTHWEST

Hands down, the Northwest quadrant of Portland has the most beer history. It all started here: Kurt and Rob Widmer's first batches of alt and, a bit later, the now-iconoclastic hefeweizen. Head brewer Karl Ockert piecing together BridgePort Brewing, then called Columbia River Brewery. Mac MacTarnahan at Portland Brewing, gone but not forgotten. Bogart's Joint, Mike McMenamin's second public house. And, of course, Henry Weinhard's, the regionally adored brewery that took up a downtown block and enveloped the entire area surrounding it with the captivating aroma of beer being brewed from 1862 until 1999, when it closed.

Henry's 12th Street Tavern, housed in what used to be the Weinhard brewery's power house, is part of a larger renovation that includes a grocery store, office space, restaurants, and shops;

MACTARNAHAN'S TAPROOM
2730 NW 31st Ave.
Portland, 503-228-5269
macsbeer.com

LOMPOC

(Left) Lompoc's C-Note Imperial Pale Ale showcases hops beginning with the letter "C." (Right) Lompoc bottles some of its seasonal beers in addition to the regular lineup.

When it comes to successful brewpubs, Portlanders seem to go to the letter "L": with the exception of the expansive McMenamins chain, the brewing companies with the most locations in Portland are the Lompoc, the Lucky Labrador (Lucky Lab to locals), and the Laurelwood. Here's a closer look at the Lompoc.

Lompoc started brewing in 1996, at what was then called the Old Lompoc; the name was changed to the New Old Lompoc when then-brewer Jerry Fechter bought the place with some partners. The Hedge House, 3412 SE Division St., a small neighborhood pub in a former Portland-style bungalow house, opened in 2003, and Oaks Bottom, 1612 SE Bybee Blvd., a similarly cozy neighborhood spot, opened in 2006. Besides a wide, inventive lineup of beers (typically a half-dozen or more holiday beers, for instance), all Lompoc establishments offer massive covered patios with heaters to extend the al fresco season and multiple-award-winning New England clam chowder. Mmmm.

Because you were wondering about the name: much of the action in *The Bank Dick*, a classic comedy starring W. C. Fields and Una Merkel, takes place in a hotel called the New Old Lompoc House.

New Old Lompoc
1616 NW 23rd Ave., Portland, 503-225-1855, newoldlompoc.com

it's a large two-story space, part restaurant and part lounge, with soaring 24-foot ceilings and dramatic modern touches. While no longer a brewery, Henry's retains a few spots where you can catch glimpses of the old Weinhard's brewery: its presence lingers in the exposed brick walls, and on a nice day, there's nothing like sitting out on the very urbane patio with the old Henry Weinhard brewery's smokestack, still intact after all these years. Henry's

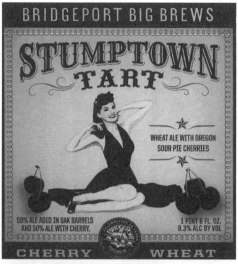

12th Street Tavern boasts over 100 beers and ciders on tap, with an emphasis on local breweries.

A former rope factory is probably as good a place as any for a movement to get its start, and that's where Bridge-Port was born, as Columbia River Brewery, in 1984. Richard and Nancy Ponzi (yes, of the winemaking family) teamed up with Karl Ockert, a recent graduate of the University of California at Davis' malting and brewing sciences program, and built the brewery from scraps and used equipment in a three-story, 100-year-old former rope factory. The setting has changed significantly since then, with BridgePort undergoing a huge renovation in the early 2000s which added a bakery, a full restaurant, and much swankier surroundings. But BridgePort's line of award-winning beers continues on.

Rogue Ales Public House is another location with a lot of beer history. Half of it used to be Bogart's Joint, Mike McMenamin's second venture after launching Produce Row. At one point, it was also where Kurt and Rob Widmer were brewing beer. Then, Portland Brewing decided to set up shop at the location, and the pub shared the space with Bogart's Joint, which was still in business, though no longer owned by McMenamin. Later, Portland Brewing took over the space occupied by Bogart's Joint, turning that half into a rowdier bar scene and making the western half into more of a restaurant. You can still see stencils of bees in the women's

BRIDGEPORT BREWPUB
1313 NW Marshall St.
Portland, 503-241-3612
bridgeportbrew.com

BridgePort, one of Oregon's original craft breweries, still experiments with its beers.

DESCHUTES BREWERY & PUBLIC HOUSE
210 NW 11th Ave.
Portland, 503-296-4906
deschutesbrewery.com

Deschutes' wide range of beers pours at the Portland location.

restroom, a throwback to a time when the entire bathroom was painted honey-colored to promote Portland's Original Honey Beer. Even after Rogue Ales took over the entire space, Rogue also maintained the obscure names on the bathroom doors: Hops and Barley. You get to figure out which one is for women and which is for men. (Hint: barley is for women because, as the staff will tell you, "women are sweet.") As is the case with all Rogue outposts, you can find a very wide selection of Rogue beers here and a few guest taps. No matter how sweet you are.

Speaking of sweet, Deschutes Brewery certainly took its sweet time opening a location outside of Bend, Ore., and when it did, Deschutes Brewery & Public House ("the Second") was met with much clamor. The Portland version's design is similar to a Scottish pub but with a distinct Northwest style, thanks in large part to the large timbers (carved by a chainsaw-wielding friend of the brewery from central Oregon) that define the dining area. The brewpub's 18 taps feature not only Deschutes' year-round beers but also a selection of seasonal and experimental beers developed and brewed onsite exclusively for the Portland pub by brewer Cam O'Connor. The two sister breweries also have a "beer share" program that allows some of the beers that formerly were exclusive in Bend to reach a Portland audience. In addition to its regular seasonal beers, Deschutes also brews up quite flavorful gluten-free selections, usually made from sorghum—a nice choice for the growing number of people who are finding themselves gluten-intolerant.

DON'T MISS

- Toasting beer pioneer Henry Weinhard at the original smokestack from Henry Weinhard's brewery at Henry's 12th Street Tavern—with a selection from the 100-plus beers, of course.

- At BridgePort, try the Blue Heron, a pale ale that was first brewed as a special release for the Audubon Society, or, if it's available, Old Knucklehead Barley Wine.

- If it's on tap, Deschutes' The Abyss is a dark-as-midnight imperial stout that has reached celebrity status. Or sample some of the brewery's experimental beers.

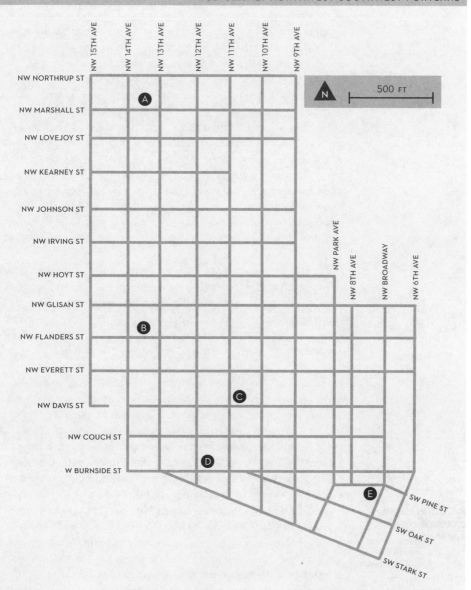

Ⓐ BridgePort BrewPub
1313 NW Marshall St.
503-241-3612

Ⓑ Rogue Ales Public House
1339 NW Flanders St.
503-222-5910

Ⓒ Deschutes Brewery & Public House
210 NW 11th Ave.
503-296-4906

Ⓓ Henry's 12th Street Tavern
10 NW 12th Ave.
503-227-5320

Ⓔ Bailey's Taproom
213 SW Broadway
503-295-1004

SOUTHWEST

A varied beer topography, southwest Portland includes several neighborhoods and Portland State University. Fortunately for the business crowd, there are a lot of good beer places in downtown Portland, which lies mostly in the southwest quadrant.

Bailey's Taproom on Broadway is a great place to unwind after work of any sort. The über-chic atmosphere, with swanky couches and a long, wooden bar, makes you feel like you are someplace special. Rest assured, you are. But don't let the cool surroundings fool you: Bailey's is enthusiastic about the beer, offering 20 rotating taps plus one beer engine. The beers on tap are planned to encompass a wide range of styles, from crisp lagers to hunky imperial stouts. Bailey's emphasizes local and Oregon beers but is known to cast a net further for unusual and rare beers. The staff is passionate, knowledgeable, and helpful, making Bailey's Taproom a welcoming harbor for both the uninitiated and the craft beer fanatic.

It is far too rare that a highly lauded restaurant features a beer menu along with white tablecloths, first-class food and wine menus, and nice glassware. But Higgins Restaurant is one of those exceptional places. Owner chef Greg Higgins, named Best Northwest Chef by the James Beard Foundation in 2002, has been a leader in promoting local and sustainable Northwest cuisine for years. He's also a big beer fan. In the cozy bistro or in the spacious dining rooms, patrons can select from 11 draft choices and an extensive menu of bottle beers, all arranged by country and served in appropriate glassware. Higgins is known for becoming familiar with the sources that provide the ingredients for his restaurant. In that vein, he has become close enough friends with Hair of the Dog owner Alan Sprints that Sprints named a beer for Higgins. Greg, made with the unconventional ingredient of squash, is served exclusively on draft at Higgins.

RACCOON LODGE, CASCADE BREWING CO.
7424 SW Beaverton-Hillsdale Hwy., Portland
503-296-0110
raclodge.com

Raccoon Lodge is home to one of the most innovative breweries in Oregon: Cascade Brewing Co. But that wasn't always the case. Until a few years ago, brewmaster Ron Gansberg, who calls himself the brewery's "chief imagineer," was making solid Northwest-style beers, but they languished in relative obscurity.

Northwest brewers started experimenting with barrel-aging beers, which added different flavors, aromas, and depth to the beers. That must have clicked with Gansberg, who had been a winemaker before he turned to brewing. Now, Gansberg is proud papa to an ever-growing number of barrels—oak, wine, bourbon, sherry, you name it—all filled with different beers. Like a mad scientist, he scampers about at the Raccoon Lodge brewery (and in

(Left) Cascade Apricot Ale has been listed among the best beers in the world. (Right) Cascade Brewing calls its unique creations "Northwest style sour" beers.

the Cascade Brewing Barrel House, a pub in southeast Portland), as he samples, tests, blends, and tastes the beers, creating an ale alchemy of a seemingly never-ending variety of complex and unique barrel-aged, sour, and blended beers that are making the world take notice. You will too, each time you visit Raccoon Lodge and the Barrel House and sample some of Gansberg's blended beers.

DON'T MISS

- Sinking into a comfy-chic couch with your choice of beers from the 21 taps at Bailey's Taproom.

- Hair of the Dog's Greg, a squash (think pumpkin) beer at Higgins.

- The barrel-aged, blended sour beers from Cascade Brewing Co., including Cascade Apricot, Sang Noire, and Cuvee du Jongleur.

NORTHEAST

This swath of Beervana is increasingly hopping, with plenty of good beer to be found. In fact, consistently award-winning breweries (Alameda Brewhouse and Laurelwood) and great pubs like LaurelThirst (no relation to the aforementioned member of the "L" empire) and Concordia Ale House call this quadrant home.

Alameda Brewhouse is truly a neighborhood brewpub. Nestled in Beaumont Village alongside a seemingly never-ending string of boutique shops and restaurants, it would be hard to pick out Alameda Brewhouse—if it weren't for the giant bronze hop that hangs outside over the door. Brilliant! Instant landmark. Alameda always offers six house beers and usually has a seasonal or two on tap. The velvety smooth Black Bear XX Stout, which has won numerous awards at the Great American Beer Festival, is worth a visit on its own. Deep black in color and just as richly flavored with hints of peat, roasted coffee beans, cherries, and chocolate, it tastes stronger than its actual alcohol content, which is 6.8 ABV. If you are looking for a unique beer experience, try the Irvington

ALAMEDA BREWHOUSE
4765 NE Fremont St.
Portland, 503-460-9025
alamedabrewhouse.com

(Left) Black Bear XX Stout is a powerhouse award-winner from Alameda. (Right) A big bronze hop marks Alameda Brewhouse. (Below) Pink elephants from another era greet patrons at Concordia Ale House.

Juniper Porter, brewed with chocolate malt and black strap molasses with a hint of juniper.

Another reason to like this quadrant is Concordia Ale House. It features 22 rotating taps and is one of those places that always seems to score the new (and therefore rare) beers first. Concordia also has an extensive bottle selection of more than 150 interesting domestic and imported beers in coolers, available for enjoyment at the pub or to take home. But the very best reason to like Concordia Ale House is the pink elephants. When the owners were readying the place to open it, they removed layer upon layer of dry wall and plaster, only to discover a mural on one wall, featuring three pink elephants, all content, two lounging with drinks in hand and smiles on their faces. A bit of research revealed that the mural had graced a speakeasy decades before. The ebullient elephants were preserved for more generations to enjoy.

Laurelwood Brewing Co. has two locations in Portland, two outposts at Portland International Airport, and crossed the mighty Columbia in 2009, opening a pub with a very small pilot brewing system in Battle Ground, Wash. Laurelwood got its start when owner Mike DeKalb took over a defunct brewpub near Sandy Boulevard. With good food, great beer, and a family-friendly atmosphere, success came quickly, and a second pub, located in a funky old house in Northwest Portland, sprang up, serving beer brewed at the original location. Laurelwood outgrew its original space, and moved its main brewpub about ten blocks east on

LAURELWOOD PUBLIC HOUSE & BREWERY

5115 NE Sandy Blvd.
Portland, 503-282-0622
laurelwoodbrewpub.com

Sandy, where it continues to brew an astounding amount of delicious beers, including Workhorse IPA, hailed as the best IPA in the 2009 National IPA Championships, sponsored by the *Brewing News*. It is consistently a favorite at all the Laurelwood locations and is also available in bottles.

LAURELWOOD

Laurelwood Brewing Co. is Portland's original organic brewery. It got its start in 2001 with a seven-barrel brewery and something that was then unheard of: a play area for kids. The next location, Laurelwood NW Public House, 2723 NW Kearney St., opened in 2004 in a 1902 classic Portland-style house, with a large outdoor patio and the requisite kiddie play area. In 2007, Laurelwood moved its flagship location to a building on NE Sandy Blvd. which once housed a dinner theater; the former stage area is now home to a 15-barrel brewery. What you can expect at any Laurelwood location: award-winning beer (Laurelwood consistently wins at national and international beer competitions), kids' play area, and inventive food menus. Visit them all at laurelwoodbrewpub.com.

Note to travelers: if you are flying out of PDX, be sure to arrive a few minutes early, not so you'll have plenty of time to get through security but so you can enjoy a Laurelwood brew at one of the two pubs inside the terminal at Portland International Airport (concourses A and E). If you are just arriving, welcome to Beervana!

(Above) Workhorse IPA was voted best IPA in the country in a national competition. (Below) Laurelwood's award-winning beers are available at Portland International Airport.

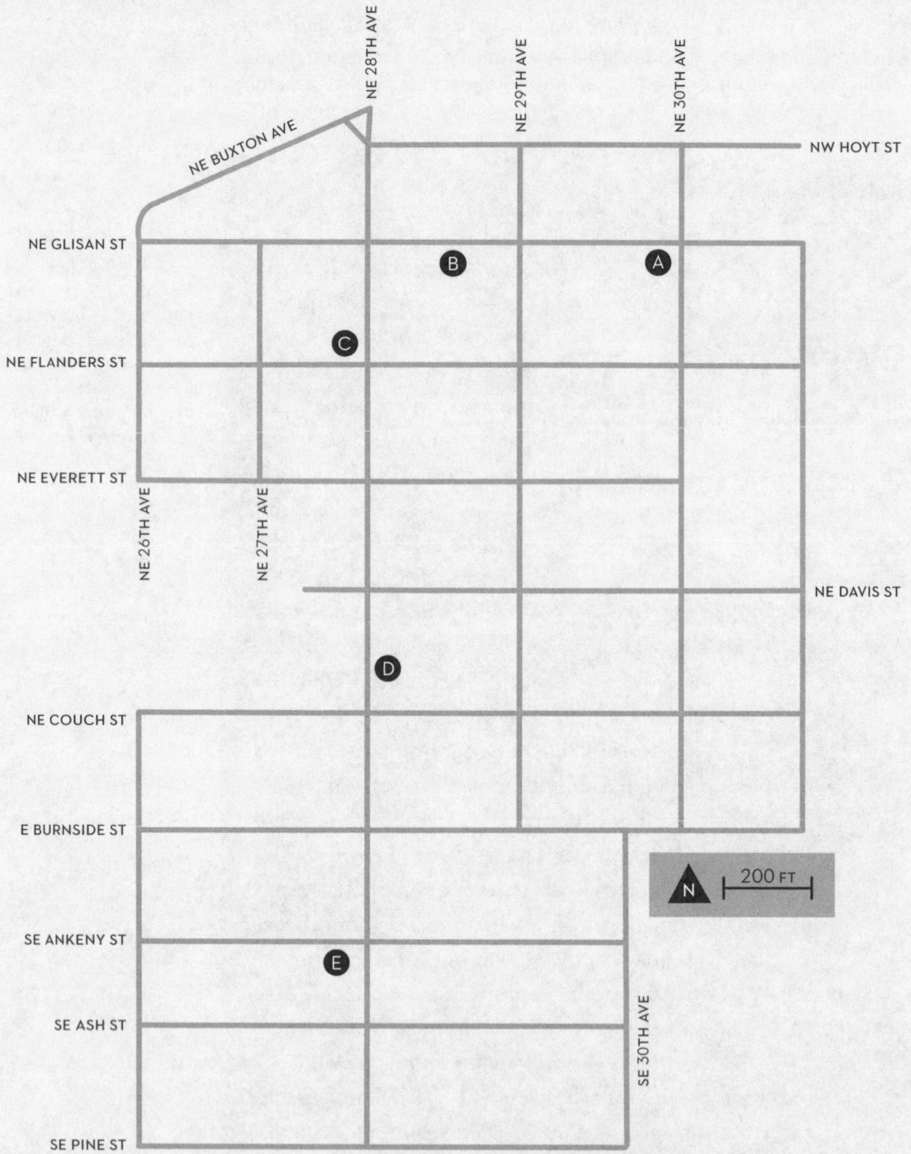

NE 28TH AVE

NE 29TH AVE

NE 30TH AVE

NE BUXTON AVE

NW HOYT ST

NE GLISAN ST

Ⓑ

Ⓐ

NE FLANDERS ST

Ⓒ

NE EVERETT ST

NE 26TH AVE

NE 27TH AVE

NE DAVIS ST

Ⓓ

NE COUCH ST

E BURNSIDE ST

N 200 FT

SE ANKENY ST

Ⓔ

SE ASH ST

SE 30TH AVE

SE PINE ST

Ⓐ LaurelThirst Public House
2958 NE Glisan St.
503-232-1504

Ⓑ Migration Brewing
2828 NE Glisan St.
503-206-5221

Ⓒ Spints Alehouse
401 NE 28th Ave.
503-847-2534

Ⓓ Beulahland Coffee & Alehouse
118 NE 28th Ave.
503-235-2794

Ⓔ Coalition Brewing
2724 SE Ankeny St.
503-894-8080

- Sampling Black Bear XX Stout, a multiple award-winner, at Alameda Brewhouse.

- Sipping on a Workhorse IPA at Laurelwood, whether in town or before your flight at the airport. The seasonally available Deranger Imperial Red Ale, a double version of Laurelwood's flagship Free Range Red, is a taste treat, too.

- Seeing pink elephants and enjoying a craft beer from the incredible selection at Concordia Ale House. An appropriate pairing would be Delirium Tremens, which is often on tap or available in bottles.

SOUTHEAST

I call this part of town the "Beermuda Triangle," because it's so pleasantly easy to get lost among all the great beer establishments in southeast Portland. So, for the navigationally challenged, let's start right off with a pub crawl that never veers off SE Division. Begin with a visit to The Beermongers, a bottle shop with a growing selection of craft and imports where you can also drink the beer. Almost directly across the street you will find Apex, a beer bar with an obscene number of taps and an equally ridiculous number of beers in the bottle, brewed around the world or just down the street. About half a mile east is Bar Avignon, a great little spot with a small but always well-selected taps selection. Keep walking and you'll reach Pix Patisserie, where they do great things with beer and dessert (try the beer float). Your next stop, the Hedge House, is right next door; it's a tiny bungalow with a great outdoor patio and tasty Lompoc beers.

Keep walking east and you'll reach the Victory Bar. Small, neighborhood establishments with great beer selections are always a treat to discover, and this pub is a gem. Settle into one of the corner tables or cozy up to the small bar and order from a nice choice of rotating taps or a stunning list of bottled beers that never cease to amaze. The owner knows his beer and is adept at find-

ing a balance of rare and unique beers to grace his beer lists. There is even a house dry-hopped gin. Hopheads looking for a new experience might want to try it as a hoppy gin and tonic or in a martini.

The Hedge House and Pix Patisserie are good-beer neighbors.

Ⓐ The Beermongers
1125 SE Division St.
503-234-6012

Ⓑ Apex
1216 SE Division St.
503-273-9227

Ⓒ Bar Avignon
2138 SE Division St.
503-517-0808

Ⓓ Pix Patisserie
3402 SE Division St.
503-232-4407

Ⓔ Hedge House
3412 SE Division St.
503-235-2215

Ⓕ Victory Bar
3652 SE Division St.
503-236-8755

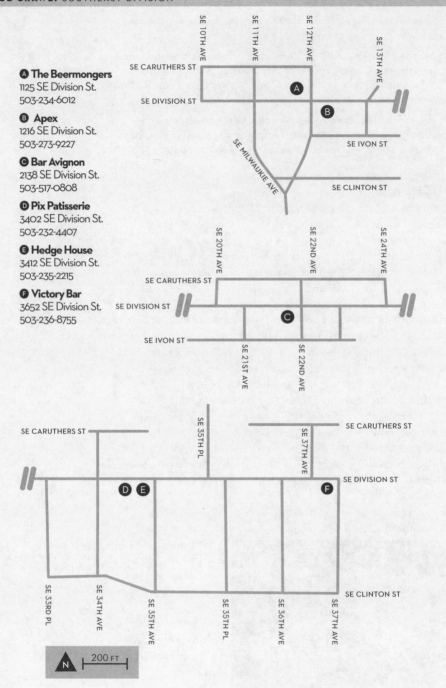

A trip to Portland wouldn't be complete without a visit to the venerable Horse Brass Pub and, if you're lucky, a chance to sit at the elbow of a man who has been championing good beer since before the term "craft beer" was even invented. If you do get a chance to have a round of pints with Horse Brass publican Don Younger, you might even catch an airing of his Zen-like philosophy. "It's not about the beer—it's about the beer," he will say in his smoky voice.

Younger's own pathway to beer enlightenment began one late morning when he discovered a certain sales receipt. Apparently, he had purchased the British-themed pub the night before in a drunken stupor. But Younger embraced his new role as Horse Brass publican, first bringing in rare imports and, a few years later, taking a chance on local guys making newfangled things called microbrews. Since then, the Horse Brass has been considered one of the original good-beer meccas, drawing fans from around the world to take in a piece of history along with a selection from the 55 rotating taps or the extensive bottle list.

Belmont Station, which used to be next door to the Horse Brass, fills another page in Portland's beer history. It opened in 1997, as the first beer bottle store in the Northwest, and in the early days also sold specialty British foods, as a way to help pay the bills. Success came soon enough, though, and Belmont Station moved to another location a few years ago to make room for more beer. The Biercafé was added at that time, giving thirsty beer lovers a place to enjoy a draft beer or one chosen from the coolers at the small bar or smattering of tables. The number of taps has grown to 16, plus one beer engine, and the bottle selection often surpasses 1,200. If you find it difficult to choose among so many selections, Belmont Station's knowledgeable staff is always at the ready to give some friendly advice. And those British comestibles? Belmont Station still sells them, but mostly as a courtesy to expats hungry for British comfort food.

When Alan Sprints started Hair of the Dog Brewing Co. in 1993,

Famed publican Don Younger, enjoying his vices under the tent at Amnesia Brewing in North Portland.

AMNESIA BREWING CO.
832 N. Beech St.
Portland, 503-281-7708

Get it while you can; taps turn over quickly at Belmont Station.

HAIR OF THE DOG BREWING CO.
61 SE Yamhill St.
Portland, 503-232-6585
hairofthedog.com

(Left) Hair of the Dog's Adam lends itself to different manipulations, such as additions of fruit (as in Cherry Adam) and barrel-aging. (Right) Fred honors beer historian and writer Fred Eckhardt—true, buoyant, wise, and joyful.

the first customer was Fred Eckhardt, a then-unknown beer writer (which was a then-unknown profession) and historian who was mentoring a small group of brewers in Portland. A presentation Eckhardt had given on extinct beer styles inspired Sprints to recreate Adambier (a style originally created in Dortmunder, Germany) as Hair of the Dog's very first beer. (And Eckhardt purchased the very first bottles.) Sprints' version, based on what little information he could gather on the beer, which had disappeared over the centuries, is not an exact replica, but Adam, as it is now known, is a wonderful dessert beer, strong and complex.

In 1997, Hair of the Dog released Fred, a barley wine made with ten hop varieties from five different countries, as a tribute to the worldly Eckhardt, whose influence on craft beer has spanned the globe. Fred is a complex beer designed for savoring; as it warms up in the glass, it reveals an ever-changing array of flavors along the way. Nuances of fruits—peaches and apricots, light brown sugar, raisins, figs, and even green apple—and citrusy hops are all supported by a big, boozy backbone. Over the years, both Adam and Fred have proved to be very amenable to experimentation, producing a good number of spinoff beers such as Fred from the Wood (aged in bourbon barrels for more than a year) and Cherry Adam from the Wood (includes locally grown black cherries; aged in oak casks for 15 months). Blue Dot, another Hair of the Dog offering, is a popular double IPA.

BEER PIONEER: FRED ECKHARDT

Northwest native Fred Eckhardt has been writing about beer since before many craft brewers were born.

Fred Eckhardt, the dean of American beer writers, has been writing about and brewing beer longer than a good portion of craft beer fans have even been alive. Born in 1926, Eckhardt got a taste of different beer styles during his stint in the Marines (he fought in two wars); when he returned to settle in Portland, he began writing about beer styles—a lone voice describing stouts, pale ales, and altbiers in a land of mac-robrewed lagers. "I remember cruising around looking for tap beers I hadn't yet tasted," Eckhardt says with a grin. "Finding Blitz-Weinhard and Schlitz in the same bar was a real deal in those days."

A clerical error in a throwback law from the repeal of Prohibition allowed home winemaking but omitted the words "and/or beer" from the document, rendering homebrewing illegal until Congress passed a bill, signed by President Jimmy Carter in 1979. That didn't stop Fred from publishing *A Treatise on Lager Beers: How to Make Good Beer at Home*—in 1969. As homebrewers like Kurt and Rob Widmer, Art Larrance, and Fred Bowman of Portland Brewing, Karl Ockert of BridgePort, and Alan Sprints of Hair of the Dog began to go pro, Eckhardt would visit their breweries, advising them on which beers to brew and how to do it. He also worked with the Horse Brass Pub and other bars, helping these brewing pioneers get their wares in front of what—at the time—were very skeptical beer drinkers. And Eckhardt's beer pairings with cheese and chocolate have become legendary (though he now confesses the chocolate and beer pairings came about because he wanted to find a way to write chocolate off on his taxes).

Eckhardt's influences are not confined to the Pacific Northwest. In 1989, he published another book, *The Essentials of Beer Style: A Catalog of Classic Beer Styles for Brewers and Beer Enthusiasts*, considered a bible for brewers and beer judges ever since, and his writings on beer and sake have appeared in several magazines. He has traveled the world preaching the gospel of good beer in his own impish way, making this octogenarian with the twinkling blue eyes an unlikely rock star.

The secret to his long and beery life? It's simple. As Eckhardt puts it, "I'm having too much fun."

LUCKY LABRADOR

Lucky Lab is a dog-friendly brewpub.

Established in 1994 at the SE Hawthorne location, the Lucky Labrador Brewing Co. is the oldest of Portland's successful "L" houses, with several locations around town. The other brewpub, in what used to be a Freightliner Trucking warehouse, is Lucky Lab Beer Hall; beers will vary from the ones brewed at the Hawthorne brewery. The Lucky Lab Public House, 7675 SW Capitol Hwy., in the Multnomah Village neighborhood, is housed in a 1925 building that used to be a Freemasons lodge; this one's a pub, with beers coming from the brewery locations. The Lucky Lab Tap Room, 1700 N. Killingsworth, opened in early 2010 as a neighborhood pub. Besides great beer, Lucky Lab's constant themes are a casual atmosphere, simple pub fare, and a dog-friendly attitude—dogs and beer are a classic combination.

Lucky Lab Beer Hall
1945 NW Quimby St., Portland, 503-517-4352, luckylab.com

Sprints takes an artisan approach to all his beers, using his imaginative mind, brewing background, and formal training as a chef to create a host of different beers, earning his small brewery a worldwide and fanatical following. In 2010, Sprints moved his production brewery a few blocks, from its original location to a larger space in Portland's inner southeast industrial area. The move answers many fans' prayers with a formal tasting room and regular hours, making it much easier for Hair of the Dog disciples to pay a visit and enjoy a wide array of Sprints' innovative beers at the source.

Continuing on the dog theme, the Lucky Labrador Brewing Co., another longtime beer landmark in southeast Portland, has been drawing both humans and their canine counterparts since 1994. The huge space (the building was formerly a roofing and sheet-metal warehouse) offers a small room for quiet conversation and darts, a side room that is often rented out for meetings and private gatherings, and a large, airy main room, heavily dotted with tables and chairs. On one side is a long wall of built-in benches; on the other is a long bar, used only for ordering and picking up beers as there are no stools. Opposite the bar, you can view the original brewery, still in operation behind glass.

But for dog lovers, arguably the best part of the Hawthorne Lucky Lab, and certainly the one that makes it unique among brewpubs, is the back patio, which has evolved from a simple space, covered against the Portland drizzle, to a back room with large heaters and tented walls that also keep out the wind. At any given time, you will find dogs playing with each other or lounging while their owners enjoy a handcrafted Super Dog IPA, Black Lab Stout, or Hawthorne Best Bitter—there is always a wide selection of styles and usually a rotating guest tap, along with a draft cider.

As dog-friendly as the Lucky Lab is, Hopworks Urban Brewery (HUB to locals) is bicycle-friendly, with old bike frames adorning the bar. Among the most environmentally conscious brewpubs in this famously sustainability-minded city, Hopworks is certified organic, using organic ingredients in both the brewery and the kitchen. Additionally, Hopworks built in several "green" features and practices: they are proud of their rain barrels (you don't find that everywhere); the brewery uses fryer oil from the kitchen to

**LUCKY LAB
BREW PUB**
915 SE Hawthorne Blvd.
Portland, 503-236-3555
luckylab.com

**HOPWORKS
URBAN BREWERY**
2944 SE Powell Blvd.
Portland, 503-232-4677
hopworksbeer.com

It's always "beer time" at Hopworks Urban Brewery.

fire up the brew kettle; and the heat coming off the pizza oven is recaptured and used to heat the water for brewing. The seasonal and specialty beers rotate frequently and are always worth trying. Year-round brews include a spot-on Czech-style pilsner (with maybe just a bit more hops, in the Northwest style); a hugely hoppy yet well-balanced IPA; and Survival Stout, made with six different grains in addition to barley, including spelt, quinoa, amaranth, and kamut, then finished with cold-pressed local espresso.

**GREEN DRAGON
BISTRO & BREWPUB**
928 SE Ninth Ave.
Portland, 503-517-0606
pdxgreendragon.com

If you are seeking variety, the Green Dragon Bistro & Brewpub is your refuge, offering a total of 49 rotating taps. Named for the Green Dragon Tavern in Boston (where Paul Revere started his famous ride), the alehouse saw several ownership changes in a short time after opening, until finally Rogue Ales bought it, in a campaign to "save the Dragon." Regulars feared that the Dragon would become a strictly Rogue pub, losing the variety of breweries represented on what was then about 20 taps. Instead, Rogue added a new bar and with it a set of 30 more taps, bringing the number to its current mind-boggling total.

The Green Dragon is split in half, with an adults-only bar on the left as you walk in and an all-ages restaurant on the right. There's also a large outdoor patio, which is enjoyed by many Dragon guests during Portland's hot, dry Mediterranean summers. A small brewery in the back of the establishment became operational in 2009, and now members of the Oregon Brew Crew homebrew club use the system to create small batches of Green Dragon beers. Proceeds from the beers go back to the nonprofit club, which has a mission to educate its members and the general public about beer and homebrewing. A larger brewery is reserved for making special Rogue "Dragon" beers, under the name Buckman Brewery.

The nearby Morrison Hotel (not—it's a pub) offers a well-curated tap list and a heap of bottled beers, plus a beer menu with personal notes from the proprietor about the selections.

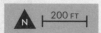

N | 200 FT

SE ALDER ST

SE 6TH AVE

SE 7TH AVE

SE 8TH AVE

SE 9TH AVE

SE 10TH AVE

SE 11TH AVE

D

SE MORRISON ST

SE BELMONT ST

C

B

SE YAMHILL ST

SE TAYLOR ST

SE SALMON ST

SE MAIN ST

SE MAIDSON ST

A

SE HAWTHORNE BLVD

SE CLAY ST

**Ⓐ Lucky Lab
Brew Pub**
915 SE Hawthorne Blvd.
503-236-3555

**Ⓑ Green Dragon
Bistro & Brewpub**
928 SE Ninth Ave.
503-517-0606

**Ⓒ Cascade Brewing
Barrel House**
939 SE Belmont St.
503-265-8603

Ⓓ Morrison Hotel
719 SE Morrison St.
503-236-7080

The Cheese Bar focuses on beer, not wine, with cheese.

DON'T MISS

- Ordering an imperial pint of Youngers Special Bitter, brewed by Rogue Ales in honor of Don Younger's brother exclusively for the Horse Brass.

- Selecting bottled beers "for here" and "to go" at Belmont Station & Biercafé.

- Any of the "wood" beers at Hair of the Dog. Doggie Claws, a winter seasonal, is a don't-miss barley wine that is different each year.

- Ordering a taster tray at Hopworks Urban Brewery; it's the only way to get a real feel of this brewery's depth.

- The spaetzle at Victory Bar. It's some of the best in town and pairs perfectly with almost any of the beers on draft or from the well-planned bottle list.

Two other southeast neighborhood establishments worth hitting are the Blue Monk on Belmont and the EastBurn. The Blue Monk pays homage to Thelonious Monk with artwork depicting him on the cool, blue walls, and a basement with pool, darts, and music; it features a great selection on its dozen taps and an extensive bottle list of more than 50 interesting craft and imported beers. The EastBurn is a light and airy restaurant, with swinging chairs that let you sit by large windows while sipping from your selection of 16 rotating taps. Insider tip: there are more swings on the back patio, where many beer dinners are held.

Finally, even a brief tour of southeast Portland would not be complete without homage to *fromage* at the Cheese Bar. Cheese and beer make marvelous bedfellows; beer has a range and compatibility of flavors that wine just can't seem to reach with cheese. Find out for yourself at this unique establishment. As the name implies, the Cheese Bar is all about cheese, but owner Steve Jones is well versed on cheese and beer pairings. The place is part cheese shop and part neighborhood gathering place, with offerings from the cases of cheeses and charcuteries. Add to it 15 beers on tap, and you've got nectar to go with your ambrosia.

SUBURBS

Relatively speaking, it's a bit harder to find great beer once you get outside of Portland proper, but there are still some good spots, and many locations will offer a selection from more heavily distributed breweries like Widmer, Deschutes, and BridgePort (and even Ninkasi, from down in Eugene), so you aren't stuck with the typical Bud-Miller-Coors dilemma. Remember, too, that McMenamins locations are scattered all over the Portland metro area, so you are never too far from good beer.

The view of Willamette Falls from the covered patio at the Highland Stillhouse is awesome, and so is the tap list. Just down the river from Portland in Oregon City, this Scottish-themed pub has 15 draft beers and two cask ales always on beer engines. Four of them are nitro taps; some of the taps are devoted to special beers that fit the theme, such as Belhaven Twisted Thistle IPA and Guinness, but most are rotating. The Stillhouse offers an

The Highland Stillhouse gives Portland beer a Scottish accent.

extensive bottle list as well, with at least 60 candidates, including some hard-to-find craft beers and a few very rare imports. It's not uncommon to find England's JW Lees' Manchester Star Ale, Scotland's Orkney Brewery's Dark Island, and several vintages of Harviestoun Brewery's Ola Dubh ("black oil") barrel-aged beers, a Scottish treasure.

The Highland Stillhouse doesn't look like much from the outside, but one step in the door and you are transported to Scotland. The main area on the ground level is family-friendly, with built-in booths, a small bar, and a few tables scattered about. The two-room bar upstairs, limited to adults only, feels like a private club, especially with the soccer and cricket memorabilia that adorn the walls. And you can't beat that patio on nice days or evenings.

In Lake Oswego, the Gemini Bar & Grill has been serving up craft beer for years. It's four establishments in one. As you walk in

Gemini Bar & Grill has an impressive tap selection.

the front door, the first thing you see is a big, open game room area, with pool tables, a fireplace, and comfy couches you can sink into. The next zone is the bar, long and sleek and offering about 20 taps. In the back, a big-screen TV keeps the sports going almost nonstop and serves double duty as a meeting room for larger groups. Or head outside to the ample covered patio, complete with heaters to help ward off a slightly drizzly LO evening. Because the Gemini has been supporting craft beer for years, it has a good reputation with its beer distributors and often tucks a few hidden gems into its already impressive lineup, making it worth a visit if you are in the area.

A business park is an unlikely spot for a good-beer location, but Birra Deli in Tualatin is just that. It's a typical lunch-spot deli, with one exceptional exception: in addition to a sandwich or the soup of the day, you can order up a craft or imported beer from several well-chosen rotating taps or the numerous standing coolers—yes, that's more than 150 bottled beers from around the world, arrayed before you. You can enjoy a beer with your meal at one of the standard-issue tables or alone at the deli, while you take in the beer signs and other memorabilia on the walls; or grab a take-out

Part deli, part bottle shop, Birra Deli is an oasis in Tualatin.

six-pack (and get a 15 percent discount). Birra Deli doesn't look like much, but it's an oasis in the middle of a suburban Portland beer desert, and a darn fine one at that.

DON'T MISS

- Choosing among the unusual beers from the United Kingdom on the bottle list at Highland Stillhouse, and sipping it upstairs in the bar or on the patio for a real Scottish holiday.

- Sinking into one of the comfy couches at Gemini Bar & Grill and sipping a seasonal beer by the fire.

- Grabbing a beer from the taps while checking out the expansive bottle selection at Birra Deli.

WILLAMETTE VALLEY

On a warm summer afternoon, you can often smell the hops as you drive on Interstate 5 between Portland and Salem. Oregon is second only to Washington for hop production in the United States, and the Willamette Valley, which the I-5 corridor bisects lengthwise, is where nearly all of Oregon's hops are grown. During harvest, the citrusy, grassy aromas from the hops can be quite heady.

LOCATION, LOCATION, LOCATION

(Above) Glorious green gems ready for harvest at a Willamette Valley hop yard. (Below) Freshly plucked hops go from field to brew kettle in fresh-hop beers.

Fresh-hop beers are a bit like Beaujolais wines—young and bursting with the freshest ingredients right out of the fields, both are an annual treat that are meant to be enjoyed in the moment.

Bert Grant, who founded the country's first post-Prohibition brewpub in the hop-heavy Yakima, Wash., area more than 20 years ago, is credited with creating the first commercial fresh-hop beer—brewed with the addition of freshly picked hops instead of the traditional dried ones. But it didn't take long for other Pacific Northwest brewers to hop on the bandwagon, which has brewed into an annual fresh-hop frenzy. Because fresh hops aren't, well, fresh, forever, the season is short. Brewers rush out to hop fields to pluck their green gems and get them back to the brew kettle in as little time as possible. Some brewers even invite backyard gardeners who grow their own hops to bring over the bines and pluck them onsite, to be dropped right into the wort.

MCMINNVILLE

The rolling Burgundian scenery that surrounds McMinnville is due in large part to its being planted up with the pinot and gamay noir vines of Oregon's world-famous wine country. But that doesn't mean craft beer can't be found in and around this quaint town.

Located in a former 1920s-era warehouse in McMinnville's historic downtown district, Golden Valley Brewery pours eight

standard beers and an occasional seasonal. Its Perrydale Pale Ale is a good example of the classic Northwest pale ale, with ample hop aroma and a light malt profile. Bald Peak IPA is one of Golden Valley's newer beers, offering a bit more of a hop presence than its other IPA, Chehalem Mountain. On the dark side, Muddy Valley Oatmeal Stout is rich and creamy with flavors of coffee, brown sugar, and dark chocolate. If you are lucky enough to spot the rare Black Panther Imperial Stout, aged for months in French oak barriques from nearby Panther Creek Cellars winery, do not hesitate; order one immediately! It's a bit light in body as imperial stouts go but that only serves to make this beer more nimble, allowing the flavors and aromas of aged wine, oak, dark fruits, chocolate, and coffee reveal themselves at just the right moment as you sip.

For years, Golden Valley was the only brewery in McMinnville. But a very tiny, one-man brewery, Heater Allen, began production in 2007. Owner-brewer Rick Allen was a homebrewer for more than 20 years before going professional; the name of the brewery combines his surname with that of his wife, whose family has been in the area for generations. Heater Allen specializes in producing distinctive all-malt German-inspired beers, with an emphasis on lagers and Allen's unique interpretation of the style. The beers are sold at a handful of pubs and better bottle stores, mostly in and around the Portland metro area, and at the brewery. Some standouts include Dunkel, a Munich-style dunkel lager with hints of toffee and nuts, and Schwarz, a schwarzbier that is replete with roasted coffee but is balanced by a smooth sweetness and just a touch of smokiness. A seasonal favorite is Sandy Paws,

GOLDEN VALLEY BREWERY
980 NE Fourth St.
McMinnville
503-472-2739
goldenvalleybrewery.com

(Above) Golden Valley Brewery brews in Oregon's wine country. (Below) Perrydale Pale Ale is a Northwest classic pale ale.

HEATER ALLEN BREWING CO.
907 NE Tenth Ave.
McMinnville
503-472-4898
heaterallen.com

a holiday beer that is a different style every year and vintage dated by year for cellaring. The brewery does not have regular hours, but Allen, who not only brews the beer but sells it, too, makes every attempt to meet out-of-town visitors who call ahead and make an appointment.

DON'T MISS

- Golden Valley's specialty beers, such as the Black Panther Imperial Stout.
- Heater Allen's German-inspired Schwarz—with smoky, roasted malt notes and flavors of cola and dark chocolate—for black lager fans.

CORVALLIS AND ALBANY

OREGON TRAIL BREWERY
341 SW Second St.
Corvallis, 541-758-3527
oregontrailbrewery.com

Corvallis is home to Oregon State University, an international leader in researching, breeding, and trialing new hop varieties, with a particular focus on the aroma hops specifically meant for craft brewers. It's also home to the Oregon Trail Brewery, which, in retrospect, was aptly named, as it has been in existence since 1987, making this small, rustic brewery one of the pioneers of craft beer. Oregon Trail's beers include a refreshing 4.2 percent ABV wit, Smoke Signal; a German-style beer made with smoked malts; and Ginseng Porter, infused with four different types of ginseng, an herb that purportedly provides several health benefits in addition to being a natural stimulant. A small room upstairs is reserved for dabbling in barrel-aged and blended beers. With suggestions of vanilla, milk chocolate, and pecan in both aroma and on the palate, the Bourbon Barrel Porter is an annual rarity that is truly a treat.

A modest sign announces one of Oregon's oldest breweries.

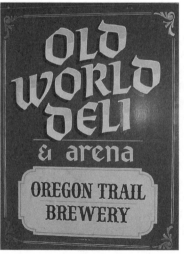

The brewery shares a building with the Old World Deli, a popular downtown eatery that serves all the Oregon Trail beers alongside tasty, towering sandwiches. The nearby Squirrel's Tavern is an institution, established in 1974 with the unlikely mission of being "a learning center in downtown Corvallis." These days, the lessons mostly revolve around the vast selection of ever-changing craft beers in this two-story building.

Flat Tail Brewing Co., with

FLAT TAIL BREWING CO.
202 SW First St.
Corvallis, 541-758-2229

a scenic location directly across from Riverfront Commemorative City Park, is a popular place to end the day or begin the night, whether you're a Beaver or not.

Fun fact: the original name of this college town was Marysville, because of its location at the confluence of the Willamette and Mary's rivers. The name was too often confused with Marysville, Calif., though, and in 1853, founder Joseph Avery renamed the town Corvallis, which he made up by compounding the Latin words for "heart of the valley."

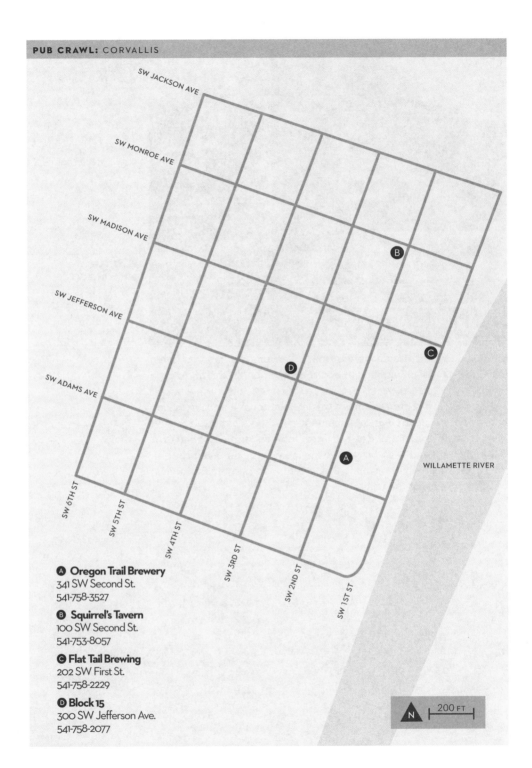

SW JACKSON AVE

SW MONROE AVE

SW MADISON AVE

SW JEFFERSON AVE

SW ADAMS AVE

SW 6TH ST

SW 5TH ST

SW 4TH ST

SW 3RD ST

SW 2ND ST

SW 1ST ST

B

C

D

A

WILLAMETTE RIVER

N 200 FT

Ⓐ **Oregon Trail Brewery**
341 SW Second St.
541-758-3527

Ⓑ **Squirrel's Tavern**
100 SW Second St.
541-753-8057

Ⓒ **Flat Tail Brewing**
202 SW First St.
541-758-2229

Ⓓ **Block 15**
300 SW Jefferson Ave.
541-758-2077

A newer kid on the brewing company block is Block 15, named for the original plot number of the building in downtown "Marysville." Owner Nick Arzner is doing some amazing stuff at Block 15. Walk into this downtown Corvallis brewpub, and one of the first things you notice is the draft list: half of it is devoted to Block 15's regular beers and the other half is reserved for specialty beers. Among the regular taps, Print Master's Pale Ale reflects the building's roots as the former home of the local newspaper, the *Gazette-Times*. Medium-bodied, with a crisp finish, it's brewed exclusively with Amarillo hops, giving it an enticing orangey-citrus aroma and flavor. Hopheads will want to try Alpha IPA, which is hopped with multiple additions of Magnum, Goldings, Cluster, Chinook, and Columbus hops. The result is a happily hoppy brew with just enough malt in the background to balance it all out.

But the truly adventurous will also want to sample from the specialty half of the beer menu, the result of Arzner's and his brewers' active imaginations. That's where you are apt to find offerings from the Brewers Reserve series (a collection of brews that have been cellared to improve and change with extended aging) and the barrel program that Arzner has fermenting in the extensive cellar below the pub. If it's on tap, do not miss the chance to enjoy Six Hop Wonder, a super-florally hop blast of a double IPA, or Love Potion #9, a fabulous fruity stout that was conditioned with local black raspberries. But based on the number of barrels in the cellar and Arzner's skills, it's a safe bet there will always be some really interesting and delicious beers to explore at Block 15.

In Albany, Calapooia Brewing Co., named for the nearby Calapooia River, offers eight standard beers and five seasonal brews.

BLOCK 15
300 SW Jefferson Ave.
Corvallis, 541-758-2077
block15.com

(Above) Block 15's Nick Arzner takes a sample from a barrel. (Below) Used bourbon barrels hold beer for aging, blending, or both at Block 15.

**CALAPOOIA
BREWING CO.**
140 Hill St. NE
Albany, 541-928-1931
calapooiabrewing.com

*Calapooia Brewing
offers upwards of 16 taps
of house-made beer.*

The RIPArian IPA, a classic Northwest IPA with plenty of Chinook, Cascade, Willamette, and Centennial hops, is the small brewpub's best seller. The hands-down medal winner, though, having garnered numerous People's Choice awards at different festivals, is the Calapooia Chili Beer, a medium-bodied offering that is richer than most chili beers, which helps to back up the heat from the fresh anaheim, serrano, and jalapeno peppers that are added to the brew.

DON'T MISS

- Making a beeline for Oregon Trail's Bourbon Barrel Porter.
- A few samples from the seasonal and specialty beer side of the menu at Block 15.
- At least a sample of Calapooia's chili beer.

EUGENE AND SPRINGFIELD

Home of the University of Oregon Ducks, Eugene is known for its active arts culture and alternatives lifestyles. With so much creativity in the city, it's no wonder that Eugene is home to an active beer culture as well.

**STEELHEAD
BREWING CO.**
199 E. Fifth Ave.
Eugene, 541-686-2739
steelheadbrewery.com

Steelhead Brewing Co. has two outposts in northern California but got its start in Eugene. Steelhead began brewing in 1990 and has been pouring its brewed-onsite beers since 1991, making it the oldest brewpub in the city. Of its regular beer lineup, try the Bombay Bomber IPA, a nicely balanced IPA with a citrus-floral hop nose, lots of malt flavors, and a strong hop finish, or the deep red-amber Raging Rhino Red, a luscious combination of roasted toffee and caramel with a hint of hops. Of the specialty seasonal beers, you can't ever go wrong with Hopasaurus Rex, a double IPA that's all about the hops from start to finish. Nearby are Rogue Ale's outpost, Eugene City Brewing, an artisanal varietal brewery; McMenamins High Street Brewery & Café; and the Bier Stein, a

EUGENE CITY BREWING
844 Olive St.
Eugene, 541-344-4155
rogue.com

HIGH STREET BREWERY & CAFÉ
1243 High St.
Eugene, 541-345-4905
mcmenamins.com

THE "SASQUATCH" LEGACY

Anybody with the nickname "Sasquatch" must be a larger-than-life figure, and that describes Eugene-based brewer Glen Hay Falconer. Glen started as a homebrewer but, like many others before him, moved into professional brewing quickly, beginning with Steelhead Brewing in Eugene in 1990. In 1994, having completed the concise course in brewing technology at the Siebel Institute, he began work at Rogue Ales in Newport, where widely respected brewer John Maier became a close friend and mentor. Then it was back to Eugene, where Glen was head brewer at the now-defunct Wild Duck Brewery. Over the years, he worked with countless brewers in the region, providing advice and sharing recipes and ingredients. Career moves have scattered those people across the country, further spreading Glen's knowledge and generosity.

Glen died in an accident while working on his car in 2002. At only 40 years of age, he had already touched many lives with passion and dedication to his craft and the brethren of beer. His legacy lives on in the Glen Hay Falconer Foundation, a nonprofit organization set up to provide scholarships to Pacific Northwest brewers to attend brewing school and further promote the art and science of craft beer. Each year, the recipients of the scholarships are invited to design and brew a beer together at Walking Man Brewery in Stevenson, Wash. In keeping with Glen's example of generosity, everything—the ingredients, the brewery, and the brewers' time—is donated, and the proceeds from the beer sales go back into the Falconer Foundation. Another fundraiser for the foundation is the annual Sasquatch Brew Fest in Eugene, a daylong beer festival and memorial tribute to Glen "Sasquatch" Falconer.

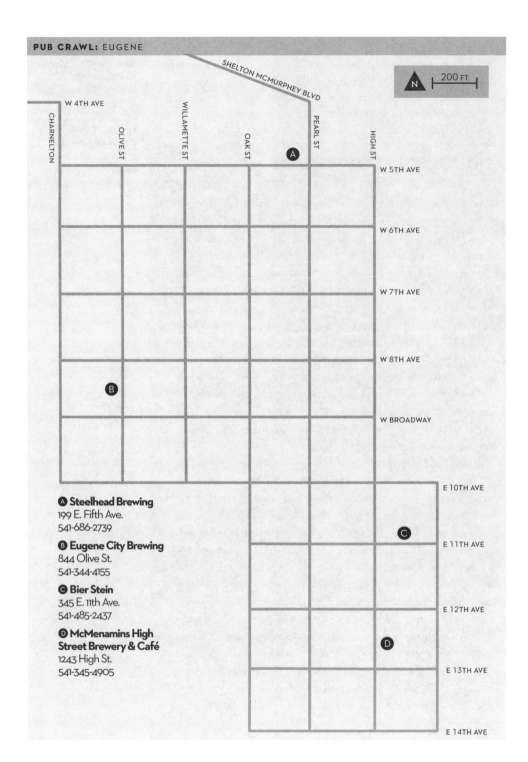

N | 200 FT

W 4TH AVE

CHARNELTON

OLIVE ST

WILLAMETTE ST

OAK ST

PEARL ST

HIGH ST

SHELTON MCMURPHEY BLVD

W 5TH AVE

W 6TH AVE

W 7TH AVE

W 8TH AVE

W BROADWAY

E 10TH AVE

E 11TH AVE

E 12TH AVE

E 13TH AVE

E 14TH AVE

Ⓐ Steelhead Brewing
199 E. Fifth Ave.
541-686-2739

Ⓑ Eugene City Brewing
844 Olive St.
541-344-4155

Ⓒ Bier Stein
345 E. 11th Ave.
541-485-2437

**Ⓓ McMenamins High
Street Brewery & Café**
1243 High St.
541-345-4905

connoisseur bottle shop and pub.

The Bier Stein is a great place to enjoy a variety of beers both in the bottle and on tap. Owners Chip and Kristina Hardy opened the Bier Stein in 2005 and have quickly and expertly grown it to be the bottle shop with the largest beer selection between Portland and San Francisco. You can grab a pint from one of the ten always intelligently selected beers on draft, or choose a bottle from the 1,000-plus different beers from around the world that are in the coolers that line the walls in this small space. In addition to enjoying the beer onsite, you can also grab some to go—a nice option because the pub can get pretty crowded. Chip Hardy is a former Great American Beer Festival gold medalist brewer, so he knows his stuff. He makes sure his staff does, too, so don't hesitate to ask questions, or let them guide you to the perfect beer.

Former Steelhead brewer Jamie Floyd created Hopasaurus Rex but left that recipe for Steelhead to continue to brew. Floyd is co-founder of Ninkasi Brewing Co., a production brewery with a tasting room that is open daily. There, you can enjoy another dinosaur-inspired double IPA by Floyd, Tricerahops, an artistic balance of grapefruit and other citrus mellowed slightly by a malty

(Above) Owner Chip Hardy presents one of more than 1,000 bottled beers available at the Bier Stein. (Below) Ninkasi's Jamie Floyd stands outside the brewery during an expansion.

NINKASI BREWING CO.
272 Van Buren St.
Eugene, 541-344-2739
ninkasibrewing.com

(Above) Total Domination IPA is a Ninkasi best-seller. (Below) Oakshire Brewing is an award-winning production brewery in Eugene.

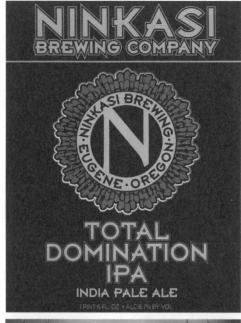

OAKSHIRE BREWING CO.
1055 Madera St.
Eugene, 541-688-4555
oakbrew.com

backbone. Ninkasi's regular beers like Tricerahops, Total Domination IPA, and Oatis Oatmeal Stout are available along the West Coast, but you can find the obscure ones at the tasting room, a stylish and comfortable annex to the brewery. Some to seek: Conventionale, brewed with tarragon, heather, and honey; the dark and forbidding Unconventionale Imperial Stout; and Renewale ESB, a very drinkable session ale with a just-right touch of hops to accent the malt.

Across town is another production brewery (with tasting room). Oakshire Brewing Co. got its start as Willamette Valley Brewing but was forced to change its name after a legal bout over the use of the phrase "Willamette Valley." Co-founding brothers Jeff and Chris Althouse decided it was less expensive to change their brewery's name than fight it in court. Many agree that Oakshire is a much more memorable moniker, inspired by the region's remnant oak savanna and the word "shire," which the brothers felt reflected the craft beer community. Oakshire's Overcast Espresso Stout is a Great American Beer Festival gold-medal winner, and Watershed IPA is a classic Northwest India pale ale, with a predominantly citrusy aroma and flavor and a gentle malty backbone. If you can get your hands on an Ill-Tempered Gnome, the winter seasonal, you shouldn't pass up the chance. Oakshire's tasting room is not open daily but will open by appointment if you call ahead of time and make arrangements.

Hop Valley's sampler tray offers a world of flavor.

Over in Springfield, Hop Valley Brewing Co. took over a defunct brewery in 2008 and has been brewing up a storm ever since. Its situation is not what you usually expect for a brewpub—it's just off I-5, ironically adjacent to an IHOP. But what it lacks in location, it more than makes up for in great beer. Because it is right off the interstate, Hop Valley must cater to three audiences: the craft beer novice who happened into the brewpub off the freeway, the locals who are looking for good beer and food, and the beer geeks who travel near and far to seek out great beer. A delicate balance, yet Hop Valley pulls it off, with a series of beers that offers a little something for everybody. The 541 Lager, named for the region's telephone area code, is a crisp, refreshing American lager that is light enough for the craft beer neophyte yet flavorful enough to please a more seasoned palate. Two other choices for malt mavens would be the Vanilla Porter, made with vanilla beans, and The Heff, a German-style hefeweizen. However, with a name like Hop Valley, it should be no surprise that most of the beers are made with a heavy dose of hops, and Hop Valley doesn't disappoint: Natty Red, a big, boldly hopped imperial red ale; Alpha Centauri Double IPA, with aromas of pine resin and citrus; and Alphadelic IPA are all solid choices for those who crave the hops.

HOP VALLEY BREWING CO.
980 Kruse Way
Springfield, 541-744-3330
hopvalleybrewing.com

DON'T MISS

- The harder-to-find beers at Ninkasi's tasting room, such as the "-ale" beers: Conventionale, Unconventionale, and Renewale.
- Shopping for bottled beers while sipping a draft brew from one of the taps at the Bier Stein.
- The heavily hopped brews at Hop Valley, if you're a hophead.
- The Sasquatch Brew Fest, if you're in the area at the right time. Good beer, good music, good cause.

Cask beers get the proper treatment at Brewers Union Local 180.

OAKRIDGE

BREWERS UNION LOCAL 180

48329 E. First St.
Oakridge, 541-782-2024
brewersunion.com

Cask beer fans have found an unlikely home in the town of Oakridge, a small community about an hour's drive from Eugene. Dubbed an "Anglo-American Public House and Brewery," Brewers Union Local 180 is the only Oregon brewery that offers a full line of handcrafted cask ales brewed on-premises. For that reason alone, it's worth the drive to check it out. But it's also the only brewpub in Oregon completely surrounded by national forest. In other words, it's hard to beat the scenery and recreational opportunities. Brewers Union Local 180 draws a lot of those outdoor recreationists who want to refresh themselves and talk about the day's fun over a couple of pints. It's the "local" for folks who live in Oakridge and neighboring Westfir—a true public house, offering different spaces within the brewpub where people can choose to sit quietly with a pint of beer or cup of coffee and a book, or join friends at the bar.

The brewpub offers six cask ales, which rotate depending on what was recently brewed on the small three-barrel system. The house beers are all stored behind the bar in casks in a glass cooler set at the appropriate (warmer) temperature for cask beers. The beers are served by authentic hand-pulled beer engines, which draw the beers out of the casks instead of forcing them out using carbon dioxide. Another half-dozen or so guest taps are poured with modern methods, for people who aren't fans of cask beer. But I suggest at least sampling the house-brewed cask beers, as they are made and served properly, with all respect given to the longtime traditions of real ale in Britain. These brews might just change your mind about cask beers. In the British vernacular, you truly get a "proper pint" at Brewers Union Local 180.

DON'T MISS

- Please sample some of the house-made cask beers, even if you think you don't like cask beers.

THE COAST

Sea breezes, long stretches of pristine beaches, artist communities, fine dining, whale watching, kite flying—you can't beat the Oregon coast for any of it. Add award-winning breweries, plus a generous dose of pubs and bottle shops to the mix, and you have a little slice of heaven.

ASTORIA

With two brewpubs and a Rogue Ales outpost within its borders, Oregon's northwesternmost city is also one of the state's most vibrant beer communities. Astoria Brewing Co.'s Wet Dog Café is the older of the two brewpubs in town. Owners Steve and Karen Allen changed the brewery name from Pacific Rim Brewing to Astoria Brewing Co. in 2005 to commemorate the city's original brewery of the same name, which was established in 1872. Time was, Astoria Brewing's beers were unreliable, sometimes good, sometimes not so good. But the past few years have seen a fresh focus on producing quality beers (not to mention the addition of some new fermenters and solar panels that heat the water in the brew kettle). The hands-down favorite beer at Wet Dog is Bitter Bitch Imperial IPA, an in-your-face hop bomb that lives up to its name. Citrus aromas compete with resinous pine notes for top billing, but just when you think the hops will completely

WET DOG CAFÉ, ASTORIA BREWING CO.
144 11th St.
Astoria, 503-325-6975
wetdogcafe.com

A lot of hops go into Astoria Brewing's Bitter Bitch Imperial IPA.

overpower the beer, the Bitch curls up with just the right amount of toffee sweetness to round it all out. Consistently a People's Choice Award winner at the Spring Beer & Wine Fest in Portland, Bitter Bitch has undergone a few tweaks over the years. Fans even got bitter themselves once when the brewer decided to back off the hops a bit. Rest assured, the IBUs were restored to their former tooth-enamel-stripping levels.

FORT GEORGE BREWERY + PUBLIC HOUSE
1483 Duane St.
Astoria, 503-325-7468
fortgeorgebrewery.com

Astoria's other brewpub, Fort George Brewery + Public House, serves up a history lesson with its beer. The brewpub is on the actual site of Fort Astoria, the first permanent American settlement on the Pacific Coast. The fur-traders' fort was briefly named Fort George when the British held it in possession during the War of 1812. The Fort George building, which now houses the original part of the brewpub, was built shortly after a big fire wiped out most of the city in December 1922. The building's huge, old-growth beams and hand-forged fasteners remain handsomely exposed and are highlighted by a gleaming custom-made wood bar and handmade pine tables, benches, and booths.

Fort George's most popular beer is Vortex IPA, named in remembrance of the Nebraska tornado that owners Chris Nemlowill and Jack Harris narrowly escaped while driving the brewing equipment they had just purchased cross-country from Virginia to Astoria. Another popular favorite, Cavatica Stout, honors Charlotte A. Cavatica, the arachnid heroine in the children's classic, *Charlotte's Web*. As dark in color as her literary counterpart, and equally as elegant, with coffee and chocolate notes predominating in a smooth, creamy finish, this Cavatica is as dear to her loyal followers as Charlotte was to her Wilbur.

DON'T MISS

- Get face-to-face with a Bitter Bitch Imperial IPA at Wet Dog.
- Vortex IPA and Cavatica Stout at Fort George.

SEASIDE AND CANNON BEACH

Just 90 minutes from Portland, Seaside and Cannon Beach are popular destinations for urban dwellers who want to "go coastal." In Seaside, a trip to the Seaside Factory Outlet Center is a must, but not for low prices on sandals or kitchen gadgets, although you can find those, too. You'll want to stop for beer. Despite its unlikely location, one small store in this outlet mall offers one of the best selections of imported and craft beer on the entire Oregon Coast. Never mind the wine-centric name that Wine Haus owner

Jeff Kilday inherited when he bought the business: he and his friendly crew know everything there is to know about both wine and beer and are happy to guide you through the more than 300 different brews that fill the coolers. You can select a few to take home or have the staff open your beer and pour it into a glass for you to enjoy onsite, either at the bar or at one of the tables scattered throughout the small shop. There are usually plenty of locals and non-shoppers there to keep you company. Every shopping mall should have a Wine Haus.

(Above) Wine Haus owner Jeff Kilday stocks hundreds of beers. (Below) Warren House pours beers from nearby Bill's Tavern.

On the southern end of Cannon Beach, quietly nestled near Tolovana Park, Warren House Pub is an outpost for Bill's Tavern, the always-bustling brewpub in the heart of town. Both establishments offer Bill's Tavern's locally made brews and a full menu, but that's where the similarities end. Warren House is situated in a quaint, historic house with a beautifully landscaped beer garden out back, a nice patio near the front with a peek of the ocean, and a pool table in the game room area. A chalkboard announces the Bill's Tavern beers that are on draft, plus a handful of guest taps.

If you're looking for a scene that's more bustling than quiet, Bill's Tavern, located smack in the middle of Cannon Beach, is a small U-shaped place that's always packed. This is where the beers for both locations are brewed. You can see the brewery, and, sometimes, even catch a glimpse of a brewer, through the upstairs windows. The menus vary between the two, and sometimes there are brews available at Bill's Tavern that don't make it to Warren House. But the biggest difference between the two is the energy level. Warren House is relaxed and friendly; Bill's Tavern is a humming hive of tourists and locals.

BILL'S TAVERN
188 N. Hemlock St.
Cannon Beach
503-436-2202

- Hanging out with the locals and sipping a selection from the cooler at the Wine Haus while others shop for deals in the Seaside Factory Outlet Center.

PACIFIC CITY AND NEWPORT

PELICAN BREWERY
33180 Cape Kiwanda Dr.
Pacific City, 503-965-7007
pelicanbrewery.com

The term "Gold Coast" has referred to various spots around the world and throughout history. There's the city in Queensland, Australia, and the West African Gold Coast, now Ghana, for instance. But you probably haven't heard of what I call Oregon's Gold Coast—that's the stretch between Pacific City and Newport, homes to Pelican Brewery and Rogue Ales, respectively. And between the two breweries, there's a lot of gold, silver, and bronze in that 40-mile stretch of land. Don't grab your shovel; this isn't cause for the next Gold Rush. We're talking medals, not metals. From the annual Australian International Beer Awards to the World Beer Cup, from Montreal's Mondial de la Biére competition to the Great American Beer Festival, both Rogue and Pelican not only enter a lot of competitions, their beers typically win a lot of medals, too.

Pelican has been lauded best brewpub several times in the World Beer Cup and the Great American Beer Festival competitions, along with garnering another similar title of Champion International Brewery in the Australian International Beer Awards. Situated on a dune just above the shoreline, you can gaze through

Pelican's Belgian-style specialty beers exemplify the quality of this award-winning brewery.

the brewpub's large windows as ocean waves lap the base of Haystack Rock, a huge piece of basalt that sits just offshore, seabirds swooping around its head. That's enough to make any beer taste good, but Pelican's award-winning lineup makes it even better. Kiwanda Cream Ale is one of those multiple award-winners, with a fruity, floral hop aroma, a sweet malty flavor, and a smooth finish. Fans of the dark side will enjoy Doryman's Dark Ale, an American brown ale with predominant flavors of caramel and nuts that's one of the original Pelican beers, adapted from a homebrew recipe; and Tsunami Stout, a midnight-black brew with dark coffee flavors and a creamy finish. But for hopheads, the India Pelican Ale is a standout for its huge Cascade hops aroma and big, bitter blast, rounded out with the perfect balance of malty sweetness. This IPA started out as a seasonal when Pelican first opened its doors in 1997, but was so popular, it became a standard beer the next year.

Rogue Ales didn't get its start on the Oregon coast. Its first home was in Ashland. But in early 1989, Mohava Marie Niemi (founder of the famous Mo's Clam Chowder chain of restaurants) persuaded Rogue's Jack Joyce to open what was then a brewpub in a building she owned on Newport's lively waterfront. The property negotiations included a promise that Rogue would always display a picture of Niemi, naked in a bathtub, in the Rogue Ales Public House on the waterfront. Niemi died several years ago, but the picture graces the pub to this day (look for it just to the left of the bar). Eventually, Rogue left Ashland and expanded its brewing operations in Newport, which is now the location of the brewery's world headquarters, also known as Rogue Nation. Sharing space with the brewery are a museum, gift shop, distillery, and brewpub, Brewer's on the Bay. Make sure to hit this last: Rogue makes a head-spinning number of beers. and with one of the most widespread distributions of any craft brewer, it's a good bet a few have crossed many beer fans' lips. But there are bound to be several Rogue beers you have never tasted at Brewer's on the Bay, too. My advice is to follow your beer muse and enjoy the rarities that Rogue has to offer. With 50 taps, you're sure to discover the Rogue in you.

BREWER'S ON THE BAY
2320 OSU Dr.
Newport, 541-867-3664
rogue.com

DON'T MISS

- Tsunami Stout for stout fans and India Pelican Ale for IPA fans at Pelican, or, if it's on tap, the Nestucca ESB is delightful. Their Belgian-style offerings are worth seeking, too.

- Toasting naked Mo Niemi at the Rogue Ales Public House with your choice of beer, then stopping by Brewer's on the Bay for a pint or two from 50 taps.

HOOD RIVER

Brewers Association President Charlie Papazian, the nation's chief craft beer and homebrew guru, created quite a kerfuffle when he posted a survey on his blog at Examiner.com, asking beer fans to vote their choice for Beertown USA. A huge brouhaha ensued, as loyal fans spoke up in favor of their various fair cities, forcing Papazian to make the call himself. He declared Hood River, Ore., with three breweries for a population of 6,736 (or a brewery for every 2,345 residents), Beertown USA.

The oldest and largest Hood River brewery, and the fourth-oldest in Oregon, Full Sail Brewing also has the most recognizable name, thanks to distribution across many parts of the country. It's also the only majority employee-owned craft brewery in the country, and has been since 1999. It's a large place. You could, literally, fit both of Hood River's other breweries—Double Mountain and Big Horse—inside Full Sail, but the brewery's tasting room still makes visitors feel at home, especially if "home" has a great view

(Top) Full Sail was among the first craft breweries on the West Coast to bottle. (Middle) Full Sail's Session is an award-winning, easy-drinking brew. (Below) The Brewmaster Reserve series features several special beers a year.

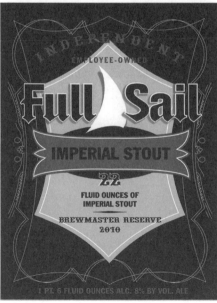

FULL SAIL BREWING
506 Columbia St.
Hood River, 541-386-2247
fullsailbrewing.com

Seeing double: beers, that is, at Double Mountain.

of the Columbia River Gorge. The taps offer tastes from at least a dozen or so of Full Sail's award-winning beers, including seasonals, Brewers Share, and Brewmaster Reserve special releases. The Brewers Share program gives each of Full Sail's brewers a chance to design and brew a beer from his or her imagination. It's a real treat to see what they will come up with next.

The Brewmaster Reserve special release series features highly anticipated standouts such as Black Gold Bourbon-Barrel Aged Imperial Stout and Top Sail Bourbon-Barrel Aged Imperial Porter. Those two beers share an interesting release schedule. When Black Gold and Top Sail are not aged in bourbon barrels, they are simply called Full Sail Imperial Stout and Imperial Porter, respectively. Because barrel-aging and blending takes time, only one or the other is released each year, giving its sudsy sibling a chance to repose in the barrel and soak up those fine flavors and aromas. On even years, Top Sail, the barrel-aged porter, is released, along with the regular imperial stout. Odd years see the release of Black Gold and the regular imperial porter. If all that is enough to make your head spin, settle in with the award-winning Session or Session Black lagers, available only in stubby bottles and designed to be quaffable enough that you could enjoy a "session" of at least a couple of beers with friends.

Double Mountain opened its doors for business on St. Patrick's Day 2007 in a 70-plus-year-old building just off Hood River's main drag, and co-founders Charlie Devereux and Matt Swihart have been trying to catch up with their seemingly instant popularity ever since. Double Mountain makes a handful of year-round beers: Hop Lava, an assertively hoppy yet well-balanced IPA; India Red

DOUBLE MOUNTAIN
8 Fourth St.
Hood River, 541-387-0042
doublemountainbrewery.com

Big Horse brewpub is worth the steep climb.

Ale, a rich, red ale with the hop profile of an IPA; and Kölsch, a hoppier Northwest cousin to the traditional Cologne beer. But they also release a multitude of ever-changing seasonals.

"Double mountain" is a locals' term for a view where you can see both Mt. Hood and Mt. Adams. Double Mountain, the brewery, is home to double house yeast strains. The brewers use a Belgian abbey strain for Hop Lava and the IRA, for example, and a Kölsch strain, appropriately, for their Kölsch. In some of their beers, such as Devil's Kriek, a Belgian-style ale made with cherries from Swihart's orchard, the brewers use both yeasts to achieve the desired flavor profile. With more than 100 locations serving Double Mountain in Portland, it's easy to find best-sellers on tap in town, but it's worth a drive out the Gorge to check out some of the beers that never make it out of the brewery's vibrant pub.

Perched atop a hill with a panoramic view of Hood River and the mighty Columbia—arguably the best location among the city's trio of brewpubs—Big Horse is often overlooked because of its diminutive size. But it still draws enough of a crowd that the brewery can barely keep up with demand, especially during the busy summer months. It started as a restaurant, Horsefeathers, and got the moniker Big Horse when the four-barrel brewery

BIG HORSE BREWING
115 State St.
Hood River, 541-386-4411

was brought in a few years later. In the 20-plus years since, the brewery has not grown in capacity (about 350 barrels a year), but with a brewhouse so small and demand so high, you can rest assured that the beers are always fresh and the seasonals rotate hyperactively. It's definitely worth a visit, especially if you enjoy discovering beers you can't get anywhere else, because Big Horse does not normally sell its beer beyond its walls. A few to be on the lookout for are Jedi Hop Trick, an IPA that deftly walks the line between citrusy hops and caramel sweetness; Phat Dog Barley Wine, a 14 percent ABV monster with gobs of dried fruit flavors; and Brother Pucker, a sour-mash farmhouse-style beer that lives up to its tart name.

All three brewpubs in Hood River are within walking distance of each other, giving you a chance to experience Beertown USA on foot.

DON'T MISS

- The Brewmaster Reserve and Brewers Share series at Full Sail.

- Double Mountain's seasonals at its brewpub. Look for Molten Lava Imperial IPA, Killer Green fresh-hop IPA, Altbier, or any of the Belgian styles.

- MacStallion's Scotch Ale and Easy Blonde Ale are two to try at Big Horse.

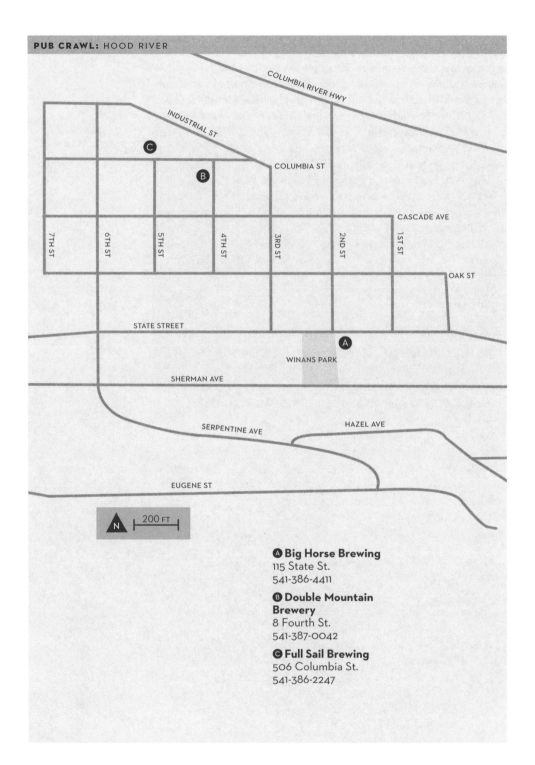

A Big Horse Brewing
115 State St.
541-386-4411

B Double Mountain Brewery
8 Fourth St.
541-387-0042

C Full Sail Brewing
506 Columbia St.
541-386-2247

MOSIER AND TROUTDALE

The tiny town of Mosier, just a short drive east from Hood River on Interstate 84, is an unlikely place to find a thriving beer community, but that's exactly what husband and wife team Barry Rumsey and Deborah Mazzoleni have created at the Thirsty Woman Pub.

The Thirsty Woman promises to slake your thirst.

The building formerly served as the town's YWCA and had also been used for storage for the adjacent restaurant, The Good River, which is also owned by Rumsey and Mazzoleni. And the name? Longtime locals remember that there was once a men-only tavern nearby, until it burned down. The popular opinion is that the blaze was set by some thirsty women who were not happy with the exclusive nature of the place.

If you're a thirsty woman or man at this pub, it's your own fault. With 16 taps at the pub and another five different taps inside the adjacent restaurant, there is always something interesting to drink at the Thirsty Woman. Most of the beers are local or regional, and all the taps rotate, with the exception of standards like Guinness. Rumsey is an IPA guy. He makes sure there are at least four IPAs on tap at all times and is constantly seeking new ones to try out. Three taps feature beers on nitro, which makes for a creamy, thicker texture in the beer. In the summer months, colorful gardens out in front of the pub encourage lingering; stay past dark, around the fire pit, and have a beer with friends, old and new. But once the rains start, that doesn't mean the end to the Thirsty Woman; you just migrate inside, where the brightly painted walls and friendly ambience warm and lighten even the grayest of Columbia Gorge days.

THE MCMENAMINS EMPIRE

With more than 50 pubs (and counting) across Oregon and Washington, McMenamins could be considered a big corporate chain. But although each McMenamins has the same whimsical vibe, these anti-establishment establishments are anything but cookie-cutter copies, thanks to the individualistic designers and artists who create the inimitable McMenamins atmosphere. Some are small neighborhood pubs; others are large complexes, offering multiple services, such as lodging, films, music, and spa treatments. Several of the locations were neighborhood eyesores before they received the McMenamins touch.

It is impossible to list each McMenamins in this book—there wouldn't have been much room for anything else. Fortunately, you can find all the McMenamins organized by location and type on the company website: mcmenamins.com.

EDGEFIELD
2126 SW Halsey St.
Troutdale, 800-669-8610
mcmenamins.com

In Troutdale, at the western end of the Columbia River Gorge, McMenamins Edgefield, built in 1911 as the county poor farm, is like a Disneyland for grownups—with craft beer. Designed as a destination resort, this National Historic Landmark blends history and the trademark artistry that McMenamins' locations are known for, all within a pastoral 74-acre setting. Within its borders, you will find a hotel with more than 100 guest rooms, a fine-dining restaurant, a casual pub, several small and intimate bars, and an outdoor patio, where the grill never seems to cool down during the summer. But wait, there's more: a theater invites you to enjoy a brew and a flick, two par-three golf courses let you practice your swing (yes, you can enjoy a beer on the courses), and a soaking pool or a massage at Ruby's Spa helps you wash away stress. Even the grounds are something special at Edgefield, where you will find lush gardens, a winery, a distillery, and an onsite glass blower and potter. During the summer months, the onsite amphitheater, dubbed Edgefield on the Lawn, offers a star-studded lineup, attracting such performers as Stevie Wonder, My Morning Jacket, and Willie Nelson.

And the beer? Well, it's everywhere on the spacious Edgefield campus. Brewed onsite, it's fresh and tasty, but it almost takes a back seat to everything else Edgefield has to offer.

- A selection from the rotating IPAs or the nitro taps at the Thirsty Woman.

- Following your muse with brews in hand at McMenamins Edge-field. On the light side, Ruby Ale is a fruity classic that many a newbie craft beer fan has cut his or her teeth on (including me). Try a Hammerhead Ale for something stronger.

SOUTHERN OREGON

While perhaps not a craft beer mecca on a par with other parts of Oregon, the southern region does offer a variety of breweries and brewpubs that are well worth the trek. From the theatrical town of Ashland to the high desert perch of Klamath Falls, each good beer establishment is just as different as the town they call home.

THE WILD RIVER EMPIRE

Wild River's establishments—four in southern Oregon and a fifth on the coast—make it easy to find craft beer on the road. Wild River got its start as Miller's Shady Oaks Pizza Deli in the town of Cave Junction in June 1975. The pizza joint expanded in 1980, with a second location in Brookings Harbor (owners Jerry and Bertha Miller's son, Darrel, and his wife, Becky, took on the management of that coastal spot); and the Miller family began brewing in 1990 (under the shortlived name Steelhead Brewery). The family's third establishment, a Grants Pass location, included a 15-barrel brewery. It also provided the Millers the opportunity to rebrand all their efforts under one moniker. The family looked to the region's popular rivers and outdoor water sports for inspiration for their enterprise's new name, Wild River Brewing & Pizza Co. Now all the establishments, even the original location, carry the Wild River name.

Homemade dessert and handcrafted beer take center stage at Wild River.

GRANTS PASS AND MEDFORD

WILD RIVER BREWING & PIZZA CO.
595 NE E St.
Grants Pass, 541-471-7487
wildriverbrewing.com

If you are heading south, the first stop is Wild River Brewing & Pizza Co. in Grants Pass, one of five Wild River establishments in the region. The brewery offers a relatively standard lineup of beers with a few seasonal and experimental beers showing up. On the lighter end of the spectrum is the crisp Harbor Lights, a Kölsch-style ale fermented with traditional yeast from Cologne, Germany's renowned Päffgen Brewery. Another lighter beer, the Bohemian Pilsener, is a classic-style pils brewed with 100 percent Czech Saaz hops and fermented with Czech lager yeast. The restaurant staff's favorite, Wild River IPA, is a West Coast India pale ale that hits the nose with a burst of citrusy hops. Double Eagle Imperial Stout is a deep, dark brew that, at 7.9 percent ABV, actually seems more imposing than it really is; based on a Whitbread triple stout recipe from the late 1800s, this full-bodied beer offers chocolate and mocha flavors that would pair perfectly with several of the restaurant's homemade desserts.

SOUTHERN OREGON BREWING CO.
1922 United Way
Medford, 541-776-9898
sobrewing.com

Here's a SOB story: only one brewery calls Medford home. Founder Tom Hammond, a Medford anesthesiologist, opened Southern Oregon Brewing Co. in 2006, after years of homebrewing for an increasingly grateful (and expanding!) circle of supportive friends, and he added a tasting room for SOB, as it is called, in response to locals' and tourists' requests. One wall of the tasting room is glassed in so you can sip some SOB and watch it being

SOB's Bohemian pilsner is available throughout the state.

made at the same time. Despite regular posted hours for the tap house, in reality the times are dependent on what Hammond and his brewer are up to, so be sure to call ahead. SOB offers seasonals and a few standard beers, which you can find at several locations around Oregon.

DON'T MISS

- Dessert and beer at Wild River.
- Sampling something from SOB, either at the tasting room or a pub.

ASHLAND

A bit further south on Interstate 5 sits the artsy community of
Ashland, home of Southern Oregon University and the interna-

tionally renowned
Oregon Shakespeare
Festival. Ashland
also is the unofficial
hub of southern
Oregon beer. Its two
breweries, Standing
Stone and Caldera,
have both been
brewing great beer
since 1996, with their
first beers sold com-
mercially in 1997.

Standing Stone is
named for Pilot Rock,
a volcanic plug near
Mount Ashland, both
of which landmarks
serve not only as a
backdrop to the city
but also as outdoor
recreational play-

grounds for its lucky citizens. The native Takelma Indians called
Pilot Rock *tsin tsat tsaniptha*, which means "stone stands up."
The brewpub is housed in the Whittle Garage Building, which is
listed on the National Register of Historic Places; for most of its
life, the space was used for automobile-related businesses, until
the three Amarotico brothers transformed it into Standing Stone.
Standing Stone offers at least a half-dozen beers (and even locally
produced wine) on tap at all times, along with some specialty
beers. The top seller and staff favorite is the Double India Pale Ale,
a highly hopped IPA with citrus aromas and enough of a toffee
and caramel backbone to support the strong showing of grapefruit
and pine resin from the ample hopping. For sweeter beer lovers,
the Honey Cream Ale is a summertime favorite. And the seasonal
barley wine, which is aged each year for months in a local winemaker's wine barrels—a different wine's barrels each year—is a
highly anticipated annual winter treat.

As of July 2009, beer fans have only a short walk from Standing
Stone to reach the Caldera Tap House. Before that time, Caldera
was a production brewery without a retail outlet of its own. That

*(Above) Standing Stone
focuses on food and beer
equally. (Below) Samplers
of Standing Stone's beers
disappear quickly.*

**STANDING STONE
BREWING CO.**
101 Oak St.
Ashland, 541-482-2448
standingstonebrewing.com

Caldera cans its beers but bottles seasonal and specialty brews.

changed when founder Jim Mills took over the former Siskiyou Pub, the space that was also the original home of Rogue Ales, which moved to Newport, Ore., many years ago. In a full-circle situation, Mills used to brew for Rogue when it was in that same location. Claiming to be the largest deck in Ashland, the outdoor seating at Caldera Tap House easily more than doubles what's available in the cozy indoor space. Both have a low-key, relaxed environment that is punctuated by tunes from the likes of the Grateful Dead and Bob Marley, which weave in and out of the pleasant hum of conversation and laughter.

Fittingly, Caldera opened for business as a brewery on Independence Day in 1997. Following suit, Mills has led Caldera into places no other Oregon brewery has gone. Caldera was the first artisan brewery in Oregon to can its own beer (its assertively hoppy Pale Ale) within the state. (Previously, MacTarnahan's in Portland

contracted with a Canadian operation to can its amber.) Besides the Pale Ale, Caldera now cans two other beers: the even hoppier yet balanced Caldera IPA, and Ashland Amber Ale, a straightforward quaff with a hint of malt to mingle with the citrusy Cascade hops. Various other seasonal beers are also brewed by Caldera, available on draft and in 22-ounce bottles, under the Caldera Kettle Series. Look for Hopportunity Knocks, a pleasantly hoppy IPA; Rauch Ur Bock, a smoked lager; and Ginger Beer, benefitting from multiple additions of ginger.

DON'T MISS

- The Czech pilsner, double IPA, and nitro stout at Standing Stone.
- Hanging out on the patio at Caldera Tap House while sipping on Hopportunity Knocks Double IPA or any of the other seasonal selections.

KLAMATH FALLS

There are two brewpubs in Klamath Falls. The original, Mia & Pia's Pizzeria and Brewhouse, is run by the Kucera family; it got its start as a locals' pizza joint in nearby Keno, Ore., and moved in 1988 to Klamath Falls, into a larger space that had been a laundromat. In 1996, the owners' son, Rod, who had been a professional rodeo bull rider, decided to switch careers and taught himself the craft of brewing; he converted dairy equipment on the family's farm in rural Klamath Falls and began brewing. The brewery,

which supplies the pizzeria and pub with at least a dozen draft beers, is still situated on the old farm, where it shares space with a few head of cattle. The rural setting is a bit idyllic; several couples have even tied the knot in the green field by the brewery, with cows watching on.

Locals flock to Mia & Pia's for the pizza and beer, and Kucera brews plenty of lighter styles to keep them happy (and off the Bud-Miller-Coors) while still exercising his creativity with some more complex brews. One top seller is the Applegate Trail Pale Ale, named for the route that passes through the lower Klamath area, blazed in 1846 as a safer route for emigrants on the Oregon Trail. At less than 5 percent ABV, Applegate is an easy sipper enjoyed by industrial beer and craft beer fans alike as a session beer.

If you can get them to sit down for a moment, the Kuceras enjoy sharing the stories behind their beers. Improviser IPA, one of their hoppier offerings, is named for Kucera's MacGyver-style capabilities in the brewery. "Just about everything here had another purpose," he says. Emmett & Anna's Pivo is a Czech-style pilsner that honors Emmett and Anna Lahoda, the first couple married in the nearby Czech settlement of Malin, which was founded in 1909. Ra Pale Ale marks the day solar panels were installed at the

MIA & PIA'S PIZZERIA AND BREWHOUSE
3545 Summers Lane
Klamath Falls, 541-884-4880
miapia.com

Yes, that is a cow in the background at Mia & Pia's brewery.

brewery, using this high desert town's abundant sunshine to heat the brewing water. Conversely, Flash Flood ESB remembers the time when Kucera braved torrents of floodwater during a massive thunderstorm to deliver the brand-new extra special bitter to thirsty patrons waiting at the pub.

Klamath Falls' newer brewery, Klamath Basin Brewing Co., was first started as a commercial brewery in 2001 by longtime friends, Lonnie Clement and Del Azevedo, after the pair retrofitted Clement's garage into a licensed and permitted commercial brewery. The duo soon outgrew the garage and purchased the former Crater Lake Creamery building, which was built in 1935 in historic downtown Klamath Falls. They opened the Creamery Brew Pub &

KLAMATH BASIN BREWING CO.
1320 Main St.
Klamath Falls, 541-273-5222
kbbrewing.com

Klamath Basin Brewing Co. has a milky past.

Grill in 2005. Photos on the walls reflect the building's previous life as a creamery. The brewery uses water naturally heated from underground geothermal hot springs to start the brewing process. Klamath Falls folks love their light lagers and ales, so top sellers tend to be on the lighter side. Crater Lake Amber, the brewery's flagship beer, is on that light side, with an easy-drinking palate. Despite its unsavory name, Butt Crack Brown offers hints of toffee and caramel, while the Hogsback Hefeweizen recalls Bavaria with assertive yet balanced flavors of banana and clove.

DON'T MISS

- A tour of the dairy farm–brewery of Mia & Pia's, if you can finagle it (please make arrangements ahead of time).
- Hogsback Hefeweizen at Klamath Basin's Creamery Brew Pub & Grill, paired with the Bananas Foster dessert.

CENTRAL AND EASTERN OREGON

Nestled against the Cascades in the high desert of central Oregon, Bend is home to a thriving craft beer culture, from Silver Moon Brewing Co. (home of award-winning signature beers that are often featured at the nearby Blacksmith Restaurant) to Deschutes Brewery, one of Oregon's largest, oldest, and most highly respected breweries.

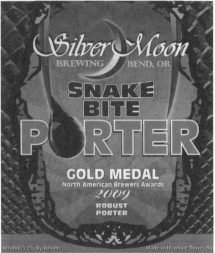

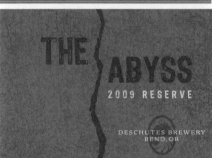

In 1988, a young man named Gary Fish founded a small brewpub in downtown Bend, naming it the Deschutes Brewery & Public House, after the nearby Deschutes River that helps define the city. The brewery expanded in 1993, allowing for growth into most western states, but the original brewpub is still in operation and is a favorite gathering spot for locals and tourists alike.

Deschutes is among the most highly lauded breweries in the region, consistently garnering awards for its brews, be it the year-round beers, such as Mirror Pond Pale Ale, a Northwest classic, or Black Butte Porter, Deschutes' flagship beer and the best-selling porter in the country; or its specialty and seasonal brews, such as The Abyss. A midnight-

(Top) Silver Moon's porter is a multiple award-winner. (Middle) Deschutes' The Abyss is consistently ranked among the best beers in the world. (Below) Bend Brewing Co.'s Elk Lake IPA is a locals' favorite.

SILVER MOON BREWING CO.
24 NW Greenwood Ave.
Bend, 541-388-8331
silvermoonbrewing.com

DESCHUTES BREWERY
1044 NW Bond St.
Bend, 541-382-9242
deschutesbrewery.com

Hop-Head Imperial IPA was brewed in response to a patron's request.

black, incredibly complex imperial stout, The Abyss is aged in barrels and blended each year for its annual release. Consistently listed among the top beers in the world, it is one of the rare beers that has achieved rock-star status, with fans waiting in line for hours prior to its release just to pick up a few bottles, only to be cellared and savored in future samplings and vertical tastings. When in Bend, a visit to the original Deschutes brewpub is a requisite, not only to drink in the history but also to taste some of the experimental beers that the brewers put on tap only at the pub. Some of the prototypes for The Abyss, in fact, were featured on those taps at the downtown Bend brewpub.

It's probably not easy brewing in the shadow of a craft beer Goliath such as Deschutes, but tiny Bend Brewing Co. does just that, and with equally high accolades. Brewmaster Tonya Cornett, one of the few female head brewers in the Pacific Northwest, admits to being nervous when she first started brewing in such close proximity to Deschutes. Her concerns turned out to be unfounded. Cornett, a graduate of the World Brewing Academy, a partnership between Siebel Institute of Chicago and Doemens Academy of Munich, has proven herself a worthy neighbor and colleague, winning numerous medals for many of her beers, and garnering the coveted designation of the Small Brew Pub and Brewmaster of the Year at the 2008 World Beer Cup.

Bend Brewing Co.'s year-round beers are solid and enjoyable, with the Elk Lake IPA being the most popular beer at the brewpub and in bottles. But the seasonal beers are where Cornett really shines. Her Outback X Strong Ale and the super-popular Hop-Head Imperial IPA, with its intense hop aromas and perfectly poised balance of hops and malt, are consistently award-winners.

BEND BREWING CO.
1019 NW Brooks St.
Bend, 541-383-1599
bendbrewingco.com

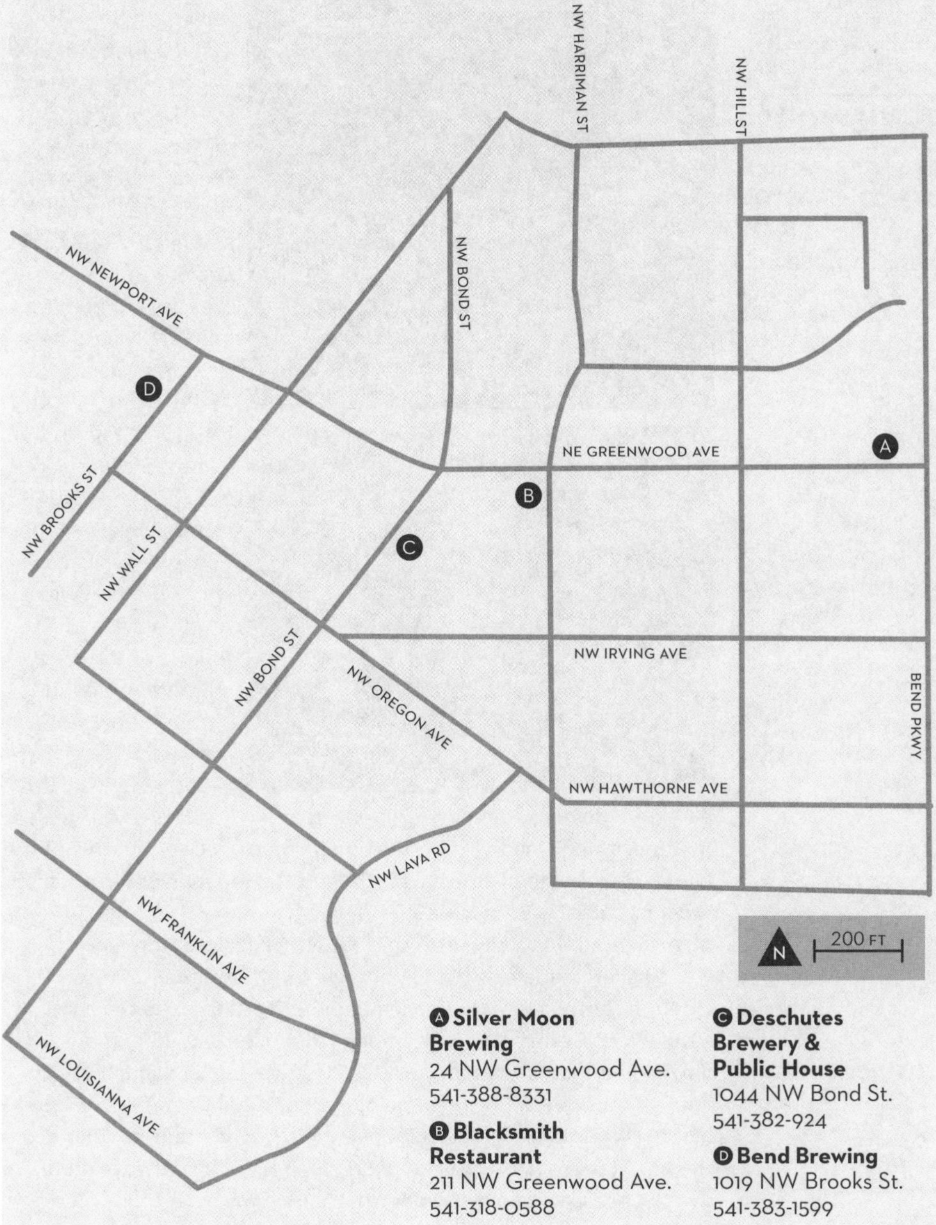

NW HARRIMAN ST

NW HILLST

NW NEWPORT AVE

NW BOND ST

D

NE GREENWOOD AVE

A

NW BROOKS ST

B

NW WALL ST

C

NW IRVING AVE

BEND PKWY

NW BOND ST

NW OREGON AVE

NW HAWTHORNE AVE

NW LAVA RD

NW FRANKLIN AVE

NW LOUISIANNA AVE

N | 200 FT

**A Silver Moon
Brewing**
24 NW Greenwood Ave.
541-388-8331

**B Blacksmith
Restaurant**
211 NW Greenwood Ave.
541-318-0588

**C Deschutes
Brewery &
Public House**
1044 NW Bond St.
541-382-924

D Bend Brewing
1019 NW Brooks St.
541-383-1599

(Above) IPA is Terminal Gravity's biggest-selling beer. (Below) Terminal Gravity is a production brewery with indoor-outdoor tasting "rooms."

TERMINAL GRAVITY
803 SE School Rd.
Enterprise, 541-426-0158
terminalgravitybrewing.com

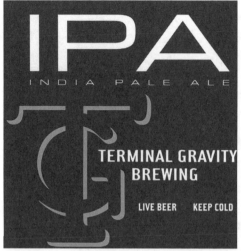

The remote location of Enterprise is an unlikely place for a brewery, and, in fact, co-founder Steve Carper says it was third on his and business partner Dean Duquette's list when they were looking for a home for Terminal Gravity Brewing Co., behind equally unlikely candidates Homer, Alaska, and Joseph, Ore., about a ten-minute drive from Enterprise. Carper says he chose Enterprise over Joseph because he likes the water better. Homer, he says, was too remote at the time, making it difficult to obtain ingredients. It's hard to see how Enterprise could be an easier destination for beer ingredients, with long, twisting mountain roads connecting the small community to the rest of the world. But Terminal Gravity has been brewing some of Oregon's most popular beers since 1997.

A perennial favorite, Terminal Gravity's IPA, the brewery's No. 1 seller, manages to make it onto a large number of taps throughout the state, and is available in bottles, as is the ESG, a delectable, eminently drinkable golden ale that offers more flavor than most beers in the style. The winter seasonal, Festivale, offers a complex mélange of malt and hops with a welcome alcohol warmth that makes its presence known near the end of the sip. Rare to find after the holidays, it is almost always on tap at the cozy, bungalow-style house that serves as Terminal Gravity's brewpub. In the winter months, the locals squeeze in the two-story building, but in summer, when Enterprise's population increases threefold, they are joined by throngs of traveling outdoor

WHAT'S IN A NAME?

(Left) Phillips Brewing in British Columbia brewed one of the original CDAs. (Right) Oakshire's O'Dark:30 was the first commercial beer officially called a CDA.

For years, both homebrewers and pro brewers have been creating a hoppy, IPA-style beer that is dark in color and exhibits some roasty or toffee notes in both aroma and flavor. Some people like to call the style Black India Pale Ale, or Black IPA, while others argue that the name is oxymoronic: a beer can't be both black and pale. Other names for the style include India Black Ale and India Dark Ale, but a growing number of beer enthusiasts in the Pacific Northwest call the style Cascadian Dark Ale, or CDA for short.

Here's why. Some of the first of these beers ever brewed professionally came from the Pacific Northwest—which is also known as Cascadia. The style also gained significant initial popularity in this region. In addition, the hops that are used to create this beer style are the varieties that are synonymous with the region: the same citrusy varieties that make West Coast IPAs so aromatic and flavorful. Proponents of the name Cascadian Dark Ale feel the term acknowledges both the appellation and the source of the ingredients used to make the style.

However, to become a sanctioned beer style in which brewers can enter their beers for competition, it has to have an official name. After much lobbying from different sides, the Brewers Association wound up calling it American-style India Black Ale. But you'll still see beers in the Northwest called Cascadian Dark Ales.

(Above) Beers on the wall: Shawn Kelso stands by a taped recording of each brew. (Below) Beer Valley's Leafer Madness is a hop bomb.

BARLEY BROWN'S
2190 Main St.
Baker City, 541-523-4266
barleybrowns.com

recreationists and beer fans, who spill out onto picnic tables placed on the ample lawn.

Baker City is another unlikely location for a multiple award-winning brew-pub, and yet, Barley Brown's has been brewing up awards with its envelope-pushing beers since 1998. Tyler Brown, the owner, was the original brewer. He convinced another Baker City native, Shawn Kelso, who was then living in southern California, to come home and help him brew. The duo continued a tra-dition Brown started with the first batch, of writing on a piece of blue masking tape the name, date, and pertinent information of each brew, then adhering it to the brew-house wall. Brown later left the brewing to Kelso to concentrate on the brewpub's other operations. Brown's decision was brilliant, as Kelso has an intuitive understanding of beer. Kelso brews a wide range of beers, and many have won national and international medals. Cascadian dark ale fans and IPA fans alike will appreciate his Chaos Double IPA or Turmoil Black IPA. Shredders Wheat is a well-constructed American-style wheat beer. And yes, Kelso still adds a piece of blue tape to the wall after every brew.

Starting a brewery is challenging enough, but starting one at the beginning of a worldwide hops shortage takes that challenge to another level. Just ask Beer Valley Brewing Co. owner Pete Ricks, whose production facility and tasting room is, in Ontario, Oregon's easternmost brewery. With all the hops spoken for dur-ing the shortage of 2008, Ricks found himself lacking an important ingredient for his beer. But a local hop farmer that Ricks had been

BEER VALLEY BREWING CO.
937 SE 12th Ave.
Ontario, 541-881-9088
beervalleybrewing.com

in contact with previously called him one afternoon with an offer. Some of his crop had been damaged by fire, and the farmer was planning to turn the field under. He invited Ricks to grab as many hops as he could before the equipment started to roll the next morning. Those leafy green gems were going to give Beer Valley a fighting chance.

Ricks grabbed a roll of trash bags and drove 40 miles to the farm. In the midst of a mighty rainstorm, Ricks shoved as many of the hops as he could into the bags, drove them back to the brewery, got more bags, and repeated the process—this time by the headlights of his truck. Soaking wet and exhausted, Ricks later that night reflected that he never dreamed when he started his brewery that he would be involved in such madness. That was the inspiration for the name of his Imperial Pale Ale, Leafer Madness, which is loaded with hoppy goodness.

DON'T MISS

- Look to the Dark Side with a glass of The Abyss at Deschutes. Also, try some of the unique beers available only at the original brewpub.

- Hop-Head Imperial IPA, on tap or in bottles, at Bend Brewing.

- Hanging out under a canopy of trees at Terminal Gravity, sipping a Festivale.

- Chaos Double IPA or Turmoil Black IPA at Barley Brown's. Not a hophead? Sticking with the riotous theme, Disorder Stout is a tasty choice.

- Leafer Madness, a beer with a great story, at Beer Valley's tasting room. Are we hoppy yet?

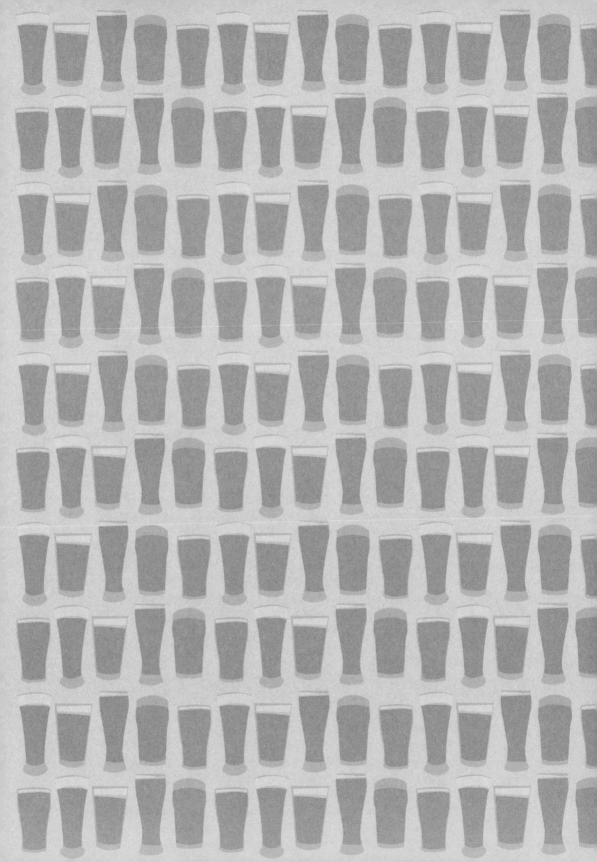

WASHINGTON

WASHINGTON

Washington State holds a special place in craft beer history. At a time when the only beer available in the United States was of the one-dimensional, mass-produced variety, Washington-based beer pioneers like Charles and Rose Ann Finkel and Bert Grant fueled the appetites of people who were thirsty for something different. Two of the country's first microbreweries, Grant's Yakima Brewing & Malting Co. and Redhook, were in Washington, and with a growing list of more than 100 breweries operating in the state, Washington remains on the leading edge of craft beer culture.

From Spokane to Seattle, and from Bellingham to Battle Ground, brewers are creating fresh, local beer, and loyal followers are drinking it all in. Even in some of the state's more remote regions, a beer aficionado doesn't have to look far to find a brewpub, tavern, or tap house that serves up a wide range of Washington beer. And support for Washington beer goes beyond the beer halls all the way to the capitol steps. While many states have a brewers guild—a group of brewer and other brewing-related professionals that work together to further their industry—Washington has a commodity commission for beer, the first of its kind in the United States. The Washington Beer Commission, formed in 2006, was created to promote the state's microbreweries, and each year the festivals and other events it organizes introduce people from all over to the state's growing craft beer culture.

BEST FESTS: WASHINGTON

Blues Brews & BBQs
Stevenson
cityofstevenson.com/brews/

Hard Liver Barley Wine Fest
Seattle, hardliver.com

Hops & Props
Seattle
museumofflight.org/hopsandprops

Seattle International Beer Festival
Seattle, seattlebeerfest.com

Washington Beer Festival
Kenmore
washingtonbeer.com/wabf.htm

Washington Cask Festival
Seattle
washingtonbeer.com/cbf.htm

SEATTLE

If Portland is the cradle of the brewpub, then Seattle is the home of the alehouse. While the number of brewpubs and craft breweries with extensive tasting rooms in the Emerald City is growing every day, alehouses (aka pubs, tap houses, or taprooms) seem to be almost as ubiquitous as coffee shops.

Seattleites are just as passionate about their beer as they are about those lattes, too. Each year the Seattle Beer Collective, a group of Emerald City–based brewing professionals, throws a week-long beer celebration known as Seattle Beer Week. Seattle's also home to several of the big beer festivals put on annually by the Washington Beer Commission. January's Belgianfest, the Cask Beer Festival in March, and the Washington Brewers Festival on Father's Day weekend are just a few of the events that take place in the Seattle metro area. But Seattleites don't wait for a formal function to enjoy their local brewers. You can find them standing and sitting elbow-to-elbow at their favorite "local" most nights (and days) of the week.

Seattle is known as a city of neighborhoods, and each district has its own personality, even though the official boundaries for some of the neighborhoods have been blurred over time. The neighborhood alehouses and brewpubs tend to reflect those surroundings, and when seeking a good watering hole, you might be asked which districts you are visiting. Because of this unique feature of Seattle, this section will take a look at the best places to have a great beer in Seattle based on the district they call home.

DOWNTOWN

Along with the Space Needle, which accents the city's skyline, Pike Place Market is among Seattle's most highly visited attractions, with an estimated ten million visitors a year, according to

Pike Place Market in Seattle is home to a historic brewpub.

BEER PIONEERS: CHARLES AND ROSE ANN FINKEL

In a lot of ways, Charles and Rose Ann Finkel are like most long-married couples. They have photos of their kids on the walls of their place of business. They finish each others' sentences. They commute to work together. But make no mistake: the Finkels are anything but ordinary. This dynamic duo has been involved in just about everything having to do with craft beer, not just in Seattle but in America.

At his first job out of college, in 1965, at a wholesale wine company in New York City, Charles began what was then the unheard-of practice of actually allowing retailers to taste the wines they were considering for purchase. "I was a wet-behind-

the-ears Jew from Oklahoma. I had a funny accent. It was the only way I could convince my customers to buy the wines." His boss sent Charles to Europe, a journey that expanded his palate and broadened his horizons.

(Left) Rose Ann and Charles Finkel, pioneers in America's artisan beer renaissance. Photo courtesy Pike Brewing Co. (Right) Pike Tandem Double Ale is named for the bike the Finkels rode across Italy (and to work, most days).

With a passion for beer ignited by his European travels, Charles started touring this country's remaining independent breweries, heading west. "Those small breweries weren't making anything different than what the big breweries were making," he says. "The light lagers with corn and rice adjuncts were working for the big breweries, and the small breweries didn't think to make anything different."

Settled in Seattle and with a mission to educate, the couple opened Merchant du Vin in 1978, a gourmet food, wine, and beer importer that was the first to offer a selection of each of the classic brewing styles—some for the first time ever, many not seen by the American beer drinker since before Prohibition. They were the exclusive representatives of some of Europe's finest beers and the first to introduce Belgian beers to this country; they worked with British breweries to revive oatmeal stout, Scotch ale, imperial stout, porter, and other extinct styles. But that wasn't enough for the Finkels. In 1989, they started Pike Brewing Co., in a spot not too far from where the historic brewpub currently resides, and the ride continues to this day.

1PT 6 FL.OZ. (650 ML)
4.70% ALC./VOL.

Ingredients:
water, organic barley
malt, hops, yeast.

OG 1.048   IBU 24

the Pike Place Market and Development Authority. The country's longest continually run farmer's market has been in operation since 1907, formed as a way for locals to "meet the producers," the market's theme to this day. In addition to being a place to pick up fresh produce, seafood, and other treasures, it's also home to one of the oldest brewpubs in the Emerald City, Pike Brewing.

A bright red neon sign and a giant beer bottle announce Pike's location adjoining the Pike Street Market. Walk down the stairs and into the cheery brewpub with its many nooks and crannies—each one painted and decorated to reflect a different Pike label. Or head to the back (with beer in hand, of course) to take in a history lesson. Owner and founder Charles Finkel, a self-proclaimed "eBay addict," has painstakingly researched and displayed collections of breweriana that follow the history of beer from its ancient birthplace in Mesopotamia to the hop fields of the Pacific Northwest, with stops along the way in Europe and other important American beer cities.

"The Pike" hasn't always been at its current location. It started down the road as a production brewery in the former La Salle Hotel, a brothel run by the infamous Nellie Curtis, the very same Nellie who is immortalized on the label of Pike's Naughty Nellie Golden Ale. You can cozy up with Nellie in the brewpub's "yellow room," which features history, artifacts, and photos of the real woman. You can also get up close and personal with the brewery, which sits in the middle of the pub, making it easy to follow the market's mission to "meet the producers." Because Pike Place

PIKE BREWING CO.
1415 First Ave., Seattle
206-622-6044
pikebrewing.com

(Above) You can't miss the stairs that lead you to Pike. (Below) Naughty Nellie's former brothel was Pike's first home.

WHAT'S "STEAM BEER"?

Although never actually brewed with steam, historic steam beer was brewed with lager yeast at the higher temperatures more commonly used for ale yeast. It was a make-do practice that is believed to date back to Gold Rush days: more than likely, lager yeast was the only yeast on hand, and a way to properly ferment the beer at cooler temperatures simply wasn't available. It is speculated that the word "steam" came into play because the fermentation process produced a lot of carbon dioxide, and one would have to allow the beer to "let off steam" before serving it.

But don't tell Anchor Brewing about Pike's steam beers; the San Francisco-based brewery has been making Anchor Steam Beer since 1981. It's not brewed with steam either, but because Anchor's name is trademarked, brewers can no longer use the term "steam beer" on their labels, using the term "California common" instead.

Market is built into the side of a hill, Pike's brewery is a gravity-fed system that encompasses a couple of stories. Also, thanks to its close proximity to the Seattle Steam Company plant, Pike is fully powered by steam, making each beer at Pike a true "steam beer," a style that is synonymous with the West Coast.

Pike's brewers keep busy with at least a dozen beers ranging from the light but flavorful Naughty Nellie to a rich and velvety XXXXX Extra Stout. Hopheads will appreciate Pike's regular IPA, but for a real IBU blast, try Pike's newer Double IPA. A bolder IPA with more body, aromas and flavors of grapefruit, and a toasty malt character, Pike's Double IPA was created in 2008 for the first-ever Seattle Beer Week. Pike's Kilt Lifter not only gets a nod for a great beer name, it has been a perennial favorite in the Northwest for years, with a sweet, full-bodied malt structure and slight hint of smokiness. Belgian beer lovers will want to sample the Tandem Double Ale, a well-rounded, fruity Dubbel, or the fuller-bodied Monk's Uncle, a Tripel with fruity yeast-bread aromas and a dry malt finish. There's certainly a lot to like at the Pike.

ELYSIAN FIELDS
542 First Ave. S.
Seattle, 206-382-4498
elysianbrewing.com

With Qwest Field right across the street, Seattle Seahawks football and Seattle Sounders soccer games keep the beer flowing at Elysian Fields, the newest of the three brewpubs owned by Elysian Brewing Co.—and definitely the largest and snazziest,

A taster tray awaits at Elysian Fields.

with cool clamshell-shaped booths and luscious interior details. It is housed in a former warehouse that had been used for decades before being damaged in the 2001 Nisqually earthquake; the owners used pieces of old rough-hewn wooden beams from other warehouses they own to piece the space back together. Anchored in the middle of the huge restaurant is an elliptic-shaped, zinc-topped bar that often sees patrons waiting six-deep for beers before and after games at Qwest Field. Good thing the bar was designed with 20 taps on each side to accommodate thirsty customers.

Elysian Fields always pours a number of its regular beers, including Zephyrus Pilsner, a light-bodied, crisp, German-style lager; Dragonstooth Stout, velvet-smooth and rich; and the Immortal IPA, a classic interpretation with Northwest hops. Many of those beers are also available at better bottle stores, so while visiting Elysian Fields, or the brewery's other two locations, you might want to look for the specialty beers that are on tap at the time. There are usually at least a dozen or so on draft at Elysian Fields. Some seasonals to seek include the always popular Avatar Jasmine IPA; the Koh-I-Nor Porter, made with black cardamom (and named for what was once the world's largest diamond); and Bifröst Winter Ale, a strong, hoppy offering that is named for the mythical Norse bridge connecting the mortal world to the heavens. Thanks to a collaborative partnership with New Belgium Brewing Co., of Fort Collins, Colo., Elysian's brewers have begun creating several Belgian-style beers as seasonals. The two breweries work together to help extend their distribution reach, but these unique, experimental seasonal beers are a welcomed side benefit.

**PYRAMID
BREWING CO.**

1201 First Ave. S.
Seattle, 206-682-3377
pyramidbrew.com

Nearby is Pyramid Brewing, which—like Elysian Fields—can get pretty rowdy inside before and after sports events: Safeco Field, the city's baseball stadium, is directly across from Pyramid, which was named Mid-size Brewery of the Year at the 2008 Great American Beer Festival.

Another must-visit downtown establishment is Collins Pub, located in the historic Collins Building, one of the first buildings erected after a fire destroyed the entire business district in 1889. Collins Pub has maintained the high ceiling and original brick interior—buildings were not allowed to be built of wood after the blaze. The touches lend the space a warm, vintage feel. Belly up to the inviting bar, or choose adjacent table seating and gaze upon the more than 20 rotating taps. Collins Pub pours a wide variety of local, regional, and even some farther-flung American

Numerous taps and a lengthy bottle list make for tough decision-making at Collins Pub.

craft beers and imports. The pub also offers a compelling list of more than 60 bottled beers that always seems to include a number of unique and hard-to-find beers both from overseas and around the region. One visit unveiled a rare 2005 vintage of Panil Barriquée, a Flanders-style red ale that is made in Italy.

Warning: downtown Seattle makes for a hilly pub crawl. To make it easier, start at the highest point, the Tap House Grill; eat and drink up and walk it off, but while you're there, prepare to be wowed by its flashy, modern interior and the wavy wall of taps—160 of them in total. Your next stop, the White Horse Trading Company, is the polar opposite: a cozy, British-style pub where you can enjoy a proper pint, a glass of mead, or an authentic Pimm's Cup, the pub's specialty. It's all downhill from there!

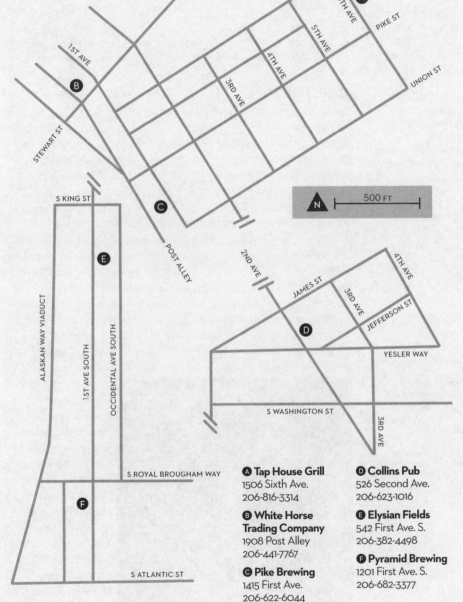

A Tap House Grill
1506 Sixth Ave.
206-816-3314

B White Horse Trading Company
1908 Post Alley
206-441-7767

C Pike Brewing
1415 First Ave.
206-622-6044

D Collins Pub
526 Second Ave.
206-623-1016

E Elysian Fields
542 First Ave. S.
206-382-4498

F Pyramid Brewing
1201 First Ave. S.
206-682-3377

- Taking in a hoppy history lesson at Pike's beer museum while sipping a Kilt Lifter Scotch Ale, Double IPA, or XXXXX Extra Stout.

- Sipping Immortal IPA, a seasonal Belgian-style beer, or Dragonstooth Stout in the cool embrace of a clamshell booth at Elysian Fields.

- Ordering a rare beer from the impressive bottle list at Collins Pub. An Italian-brewed sour Flanders-style red ale, anyone?

CAPITOL HILL

ELYSIAN BREWING CO.
1221 E. Pike St.
Seattle, 206-860-1920
elysianbrewing.com

SIX ARMS
300 E. Pike St.
Seattle, 206-223-1698
mcmenamins.com

"Monk" is a word often associated with Belgian-style beers: Trappist monks still brew in Belgium.

You will definitely want to plan on walking in Capitol Hill as much as possible. The densely populated area has mostly on-street parking, which is almost always taken up by residents who live in the surrounding apartments and seemingly never move their vehicles. This neighborhood boasts the original Elysian Brewing Co., with 16 Elysian beers on tap, including a nice selection of rotating seasonals. Barca, with nearly 30 taps (some that rotate by style or brewery), offers a wide selection of both local and worldwide brews. Quinn's is a well-respected gastropub that has a good reputation for both its food menu and the dozen-plus beers on tap. Six Arms, named for the sculpture of a multi-armed Hindu god that graces the premises, is a tiny brewery shoehorned into a typically eclectic McMenamins space; Six Arms was the birthplace of one of McMenamins' popular beers, Proletariat Porter.

But a beer excursion to Capitol Hill is not complete without a trip to the Stumbling Monk. This tiny, darkly lit bar opens at 6 p.m., when parking is especially a nightmare; still, it manages to be at the top of visiting beer fans' must-see lists in Seattle. It's also a laid-back neighborhood hangout, with locals drinking up the dark, brooding atmosphere along with Belgian and American draft and bottled beers. The owners started the Monk as a bottle shop, and it's easy to see that passion

still alive in the ever-changing, actively curated bottle list. The space—previously a typewriter repair shop—is so small, it takes only one bartender to cover the entire bar. When the servers are not pouring beer, you can often catch them meticulously wiping lipstick and fingerprints from bused beer glasses before sending them to the dishwasher, an impressive level of attention to detail.

The chalkboard draft list is divided between American and Belgian beers—five of each—with tiny icons indicating the type of glass (chalice, tulip, and such) the beer will be served in sketched beside each entry. Despite having only ten beers available on draft, the list is always well thought out and usually offers the full spectrum, something in the light and refreshing mode all the way to the big, full, high-alcohol sippers. The bottle list is also written on an easily updated board, but this time is split between "Belgian" (which also includes Belgian-style beers) and "Other," which can range from a local oak-aged imperial stout to an eastern Washington IPA. With more than 30 bottled beers on this hand-chosen list, there's sure to be something for every palate—and heaven for Belgian beer fans.

The best way to find a nearby place to have a beer is to ask the people at the current pub, and the owners and bartender at the Monk guided me to Summit Public House, just a few blocks away. They were right. Summit is a friendly neighborhood pub with a solid selection of beers on rotating taps, which means there is almost always something new as soon as another keg is tapped. The draft beers tend to be more unusual than the regular fare, which keeps things interesting. If you have questions about the beers, ask the bartenders. One time, the server steered me away from a beer he didn't think was up to par and gave me a sample of something he thought I should try instead. He was right.

Similarly, the clientele is very friendly, mostly neighbors who walk there from their nearby homes for a beer and to play some free pool. You get the feeling you could be a regular there yourself after the first visit. As at the Stumbling Monk, there is no kitchen, but the folks at Summit don't mind if you bring something in—as long as you bring enough for them!

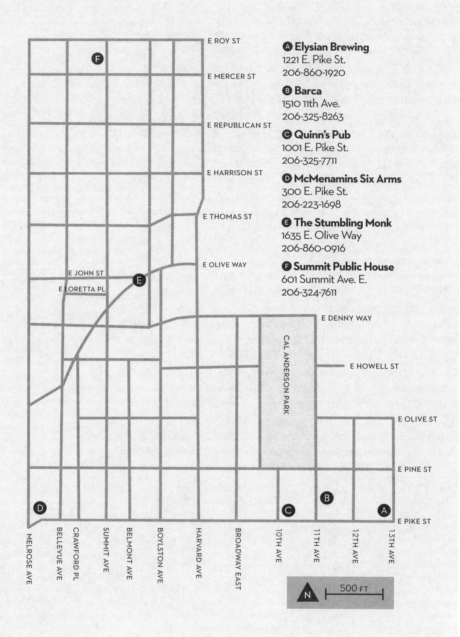

A Elysian Brewing
1221 E. Pike St.
206-860-1920

B Barca
1510 11th Ave.
206-325-8263

C Quinn's Pub
1001 E. Pike St.
206-325-7711

D McMenamins Six Arms
300 E. Pike St.
206-223-1698

E The Stumbling Monk
1635 E. Olive Way
206-860-0916

F Summit Public House
601 Summit Ave. E.
206-324-7611

DON'T MISS

- Choosing from the darkly lit selections constantly updated on the chalkboard at Stumbling Monk.

- Proletariat Porter at tiny McMenamins Six Arms.

- Chatting up the locals and the friendly bartenders at Summit Public House.

FREMONT-BALLARD

The Fremont-Ballard neighborhood is rich with great places to grab a beer, but four are real standouts for completely different reasons: Hale's Ales for its history, the Dray for cramming a lot in a little package, Maritime Pacific Brewing's Jolly Roger Taproom for its deservedly loyal following, and Brouwer's Café for the respect it brings to the beer culture.

Hale's Ales has been around since 1983. Founder Mike Hale had recently returned home from a trip abroad, where he'd become enamored with European beers. His first brewery was a production facility in Colville; he opened a second brewery in Kirkland a few years later, and then moved the first to Spokane in 1991. All brewing operations were consolidated in the mid-1990s when Hale's moved to the Ballard district. The brewery is housed in a former industrial hose manufacturing plant; the brewpub opened at the same time.

The 30-barrel, steam-heated brewing system can be seen from part of the pub, where cozy leather couches invite you to sit and

watch the brewing process. Or step inside the actual pub, where a classic bar made of Honduran mahogany is the centerpiece, sporting numerous taps from which servers pour a variety of Hale's Ales. Try the award-winning Cream Ale or, on the darker side but just as smooth, the Cream Stout. The hoppy, fuller flavored Red Menace Big

HALE'S ALES
4301 Leary Way NW
Seattle, 206-706-1544
halesbrewery.com

Hale's Ales has been brewing craft beer since 1983, but not always in the Ballard district.

Amber is not your typical amber, with a heavy dose of 100 percent Centennial hops. The Troll Porter is a robust, Northwest version of the style, and Super Mongoose IPA is a hoppier, maltier version of Hale's regular Mongoose IPA, with more of everything that makes a Northwest IPA taste so good.

JOLLY ROGER TAPROOM, MARITIME PACIFIC BREWING CO.
1111 NW Ballard Way
Seattle, 206-782-6181

Just up the road a bit is the Jolly Roger Taproom, a nautical-themed hideaway connected to Maritime Pacific Brewing Co. Both the brewery and the pub were moved in 2010 to a larger facility, expanding both brewery and tap house. The expansion took longer than expected, leaving fans waiting for their Jolly Roger fix for months. But as soon as the pub opened, it was again elbow to elbow with loyal customers, despite the extra space. Loyal patrons recommend the Islander Pale Ale Dry-Hopped (aka "the dry-hopped"), with an extra boost of whole-leaf Cascade hops added to each keg. The result is an assertive lemony citrus aroma and

A sampler tray is a good way to get the flavor of Maritime Pacific's beers.

flavor. Crisp and citrusy, with a nice malt balance, the Imperial Pale Ale is also a hophead's dream. I always like to sample a brewery's pilsner if they have one, as there is very little room for error in that style. Maritime Pacific's Portage Bay Pilsener speaks to great brewing practices; it is a well-crafted northern European–style lager, rich in flavor with a crisp, clean finish.

The Dray, tiny and charming, with a great draft and bottle list, is proof that good things come in small packages. The name is a clever double entendre. A dray is a type of cart that was once used to move heavy items such as beer barrels, but it is also a word for a squirrel's nest. Owner Jamie Butler once had a pet squirrel named Steve, and the Dray's woodsy theme, complete with paneled walls, and tables and bar stools made from tree trunks, is a tribute to Steve. Try counting the squirrels—stuffed, painted, and plastic—as you sip your beer. This cozy space has 13 taps, all well chosen and listed on the printed beer menu by beer color, from light to dark. Despite the Dray's diminutive dimensions, the beers cycle through so quickly that it's rare to find the same brews on tap twice in a row. There's also a list of more than 100 bottled beers. The emphasis, both draft and bottle, is on Northwest and

(Above) One step into Brouwer's Café transports you to Brussels (Below) Matt Bonney keeps tabs on the taps at Brouwer's Café.

Belgian beers, but you are sure to find something unexpected every time you decide to nestle into the Dray.

On the opposite end of the scale is Brouwer's Café. You could probably fit three versions of the Dray into this spacious setting, especially if you include the horseshoe-shaped loft area that rims the main floor. Co-founder Matt Bonney says the main goal of Brouwer's Café is to legitimize beer so that it is appreciated and respected at the same level as wine, while still making it approachable to the average consumer, an objective that is achieved at every turn. Bonney and co-founder Matt Vandenberghe both appreciate Belgian beers and have made numerous trips to Belgium to explore its unique beer culture. Brouwer's Café reflects their admiration, from the array of Belgian beers on tap and in bottles to the proper usage of glassware and the classic Belgian food, including mussels and *frites*, on the menu. There's even a replica of Brussels' landmark statue, "Manneken Pis," greeting patrons as they enter.

Much like the Wizard of Oz, the magic of Brouwer's takes place "behind the curtain." In this case, though, the curtain is the wall of 62 taps, behind which is a large cooler where the beer is stored for both cellaring and pouring. One side of the cooler is set at 52 degrees for beer storage; that's where you find kegs and barrels and box upon box of bottled beers. The other side, for the beers that are being poured, is kept at 42 degrees; on that side, kegs line up against the wall, and an ordered tangle of tap lines runs directly from each keg through the wall and out to a tap on the other side. Clean tap lines are an important part of serving beer, as beer stored in lines can begin to influence the flavor. Any establishment that cares about beer will clean its tap lines regularly, using a cleaning agent that runs through the plastic lines. But at Brouwer's Café, they never clean the tap lines; they simply replace them with new lines, a procedure that eliminates nearly all instances of off flavors in the beer.

The same attention to detail takes place on the outside of the cooler, with every glass of beer poured at Brouwer's. Much like a sommelier at a wine-focused restaurant, servers are required to know the flavor profile, bittering level, alcohol content, and other pertinent information for each beer that is served at Brouwer's so they can assist patrons in selecting a perfect beer for their meal, their mood, or their palate. Wait staff are given monthly take-home beer tests designed not only to help them improve their knowledge but to inspire them to learn more, so they can better serve and instruct their customers.

The attention to detail continues with each beer order placed.

Appropriate glassware is selected and set upon a "rinser," which sprays water into the inside of the vessel. The rinser showers away any impurities and, according to Bonney, softens the glass so that it doesn't cause any further agitation to the beer. The beer is then poured with a vigorous head and any extra foam is shaved off the top of the glass with a blunt knife, making the head flush with the rim of the glass. Finally, the glass is dunked briefly in a water bath to remove any excess beer from its exterior before it reaches the customer. Sure, it's a lot of extra steps, but you sure feel like the beer in your glass is special. It is, and that's what Brouwer's Café is all about.

One likely pub crawl starts in Ballard but dips into the Phinney Ridge neighborhood for the last few stops. Barking Dog Alehouse is a neighborhood pub with about 20 rotating taps—three of which are specialty taps that pour Belgian and Belgian-style beers; it also has a well-selected bottle list of about 30 different imported beers and cider. The Reading Gaol Pub was named for the poem that Oscar Wilde wrote while he was incarcerated in the institution of the same name; this "redding jail," as it is pronounced, is a lot more pleasant. Raise a toast to Mr. Wilde from a selection of 17 well-planned taps. A stretch away but worth the crawl is Sully's Snowgoose Saloon—look for the English-style cottage that looks like it might serve Hobbits (but don't worry, they actually serve beer instead). The Park Pub is kitty-corner from Sully's. Both are neighborhood haunts that have good beer selections.

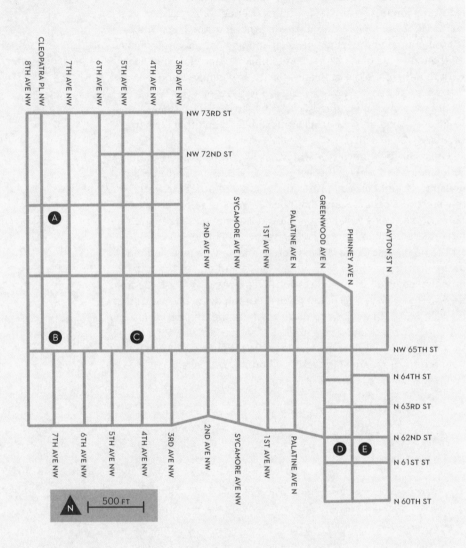

A Barking Dog Alehouse
705 NW 70th St.
206-782-2974

B The Dray
708 NW 65th St.
206-453-4527

C Reading Gaol Pub
418 NW 65th St.
206-783-3002

D Sully's Snow-goose Saloon
6119 Phinney
Ave. N.
206-782-9231

E The Park Pub
6114 Phinney
Ave. N.
206-789-8187

- The Super Mongoose IPA or the Cream Stout on nitro at Hale's.

- "The dry-hopped" at the Jolly Roger Taproom.

- Counting squirrels while sipping a beer from more than 100 choices at the Dray.

- Watching the server give your beer the full treatment at Brouwer's Café.

GREEN LAKE-WALLINGFORD-PHINNEY RIDGE

Before Matt Bonney and Matt Vandenberghe brought Brouwer's Café to Fremont-Ballard, they started Bottleworks, a beer bottle shop. Opened in 1999, Bottleworks has grown into one of the country's premier bottle shops, with more than 950 bottles of

Bottleworks' knowledge-able staff can pour you a beer while you browse for bottles.

domestic craft, imported, and vintage beers. Each staff member is at the ready to help you find the beer you are looking for, whether it's a beer you didn't quite get the name of while on vacation in Europe or one to complement a special dinner. That was great, but Bottleworks then added five taps in the corner of the diminutive store so that you can sip a great beer while shopping for some, adding a new dimension to the experience. As one would guess from the surroundings, these five taps are always stellar selections. The staff can even fill up a growler of beer from one of the taps so you can take it to go. Often, there will be a beer brewed especially for Bottleworks on tap or in the bottle. Artisan breweries across the country have been known to develop and brew a exclusive beer to honor Bottlworks, especially on its anniversaries.

That status isn't reserved just for Bottleworks, though. Brewers have also made special beers in tribute to the Latona Pub. Rogue Ales, of Newport, Ore., created a specially labeled beer for the Latona when head brewer John Maier visited there for a special event. On its twenty-second anniversary, the brewers at Elysian

The bottle list at Über Tavern rivals those in Belgium for variety and selection.

created a special birthday brew for Latona named The DeLorean. Numbering only 11, the Latona's taps might not be as numerous as other locations, but they always feature an intelligently selected and diverse lineup, mostly from the Northwest. The friendly staff knows their beer, and the relaxing neighborhood atmosphere will draw you in again and again. The Latona is a sister pub to the Hopvine and the Fiddler's Inn, all three of which share a well-founded appreciation for good beer.

The Duck Island Ale House can feel, simultaneously, like a gritty dive bar, a craft beer haven, and a neighborhood hangout. The fact is, it's a bit of all three, packed into a small space. But once you've entered, and you take note of the great beers on tap, along with a small but well-planned selection of bottles, you realize that this Green Lake pub's ugly duckling exterior hides a beautiful swan. Friendly bartenders can help you navigate the 20 or so taps, which always feature at least a few offerings that will take you by surprise. Another source of astonishment is the tap collection that hangs from the ceiling. Hundreds of different tap handles hover above, like so many constellations of UFOs, tending to give you a sense of vertigo even before you have taken a sip from your beer. Hungry? You can order anything from the neighboring Beth's Café, which has been featured on the Food Network, and someone will bring the food to you. With so much going for it, the Duck is an easy habit to fall into. You, like others before you, might just find yourself "stuck on the Duck."

Another must-visit beer destination, the Über Tavern, is just a short walk from the Duck. Owned by Rick Carpenter, who organizes both the Seattle International and Portland International beer festivals, Über Tavern features beers from around the world but also pays homage to American and Northwest craft brewers on its 20-plus taps. Most of those are rotating taps. One exception is Delirium Tremens, a highly respected Belgian beer that has its own tap, complete with a small 3D replica of the beer label's iconic pink elephant sitting on top. The ample bar is a great place to get some information on the beers from the informative staff and peruse the extensive list of 200-plus different bottled beers, but it's hard to resist sitting at the big, tabletop fire pit that takes up a good portion of the tiny room. Like its neighbor, the Duck, Über doesn't have any food, but you can bring in your own or order delivery from nearby restaurants; they even keep a notebook with menus on hand for just such occasions.

DON'T MISS

- Beers created by a host of esteemed breweries (Hair of the Dog and New Belgium, for example) especially for Bottleworks. Grab a glass of one of the beers on tap at the store while shopping.

- Ordering a bite from renowned Beth's Café while appreciating a draft beer from the eye-popping selection at Duck Island.

- Sitting at the bar or the fire-pit table and sipping Delirium Tremens straight from the pink elephant tap at Über Tavern.

GREENWOOD-BROADVIEW

What happens when the brewery isn't quite ready to be fully operational, but the rest of the brewpub is? Often, brewers will open with a full lineup of guest taps to get people in the doors while the brewery and beer recipes are still being tweaked. Then, when the house beers are ready, the guest taps are replaced by the beers made onsite.

In the case of Naked City Brewery & Taphouse, though, the original plan was always to offer an impressive selection of guest taps right alongside Naked City's beers. When the brewery got up and running, Naked City's beers simply were added to the mix of the already remarkable lineup of 24 rotating taps, plus one cider and a root beer. The draft list usually emphasizes small, innovative brewers, mostly from the West Coast, but includes others from

Naked City's Big Lebrewski tap handle ties the room together. The beer is good, too.

NAKED CITY BREWERY & TAPHOUSE
8564 Greenwood Ave. N.
Seattle, 206-838-6299
nakedcitybrewing.com

Pillager's Pub owner Jeff Smiley demonstrates Das Boot.

across America and a few imports. Because one of the owners used to work for a large software company that is based in the Seattle area, Naked City takes advantage of technology: customers can get a real-time alert through a computer or cell phone each time a new keg is tapped.

Depending on how busy the brewers have been in the small, three-barrel system, Naked City's beers take up about four of those taps, give or take a tap or two. The Big Lebrewski, a tasty, 12 percent ABV imperial milk stout, is a house favorite—and not just because the tap handle is a bobblehead of "The Dude" from the movie *The Big Lebowski.* Speaking of movies, the name Naked City, which has raised more than one eyebrow, comes from the 1948 film noir of the same name. Co-owner Don Webb is a big classic film buff; movie paraphernalia, including an original ad for *Naked City*, is scattered throughout the pub, and a TV at the bar is usually set to a classic movie channel instead of the ubiquitous sports networks. It's not every day you get to say you had a beer with Henry Fonda or Kate Hepburn.

You can use Naked City as the starting point of a pub crawl for the navigationally challenged that takes you to four locations on one street. Kitty-corner from Naked City is Pillager's Pub, a pirate-themed outpost for Baron Brewing's German-inspired beers and its other line of brews, Three Skulls, plus a few well-chosen guest taps. In the Baron line, try the crisp, northern European–style pilsner, the slightly roasty and dark schwarzbier, and the hearty doppelbock. Baron's Three Skulls lineup offers more typical American craft beer styles—an IPA, a pale ale, a porter, and more. The Black Bonney Porter, and the barley wine, aptly named Wreckage, are two that are worth a try. If the number in your party is three or more and you are feeling adventurous, order your beer in Das Boot, the boot-shaped drinking vessel that was featured in the movie *Beerfest*. But be warned: the house rule is you can pass the boot, but you can't set it down until it's empty. Insider tip: make sure to turn the boot so the toe faces the side, not up or down, else you'll be wearing the beer instead of drinking it.

Just down Greenwood is the 74th Street Ale House, where you'll find a solid variety among the 15 predominantly local taps, including cider and a few British and Irish beers. The pub has only one rotating tap, but it changes every time a keg runs out.

You will want to get your oompah on for the next stop. Prost! Tavern, the original location for this German-themed family of pubs, offers ten taps, all imported from Germany and served in the appropriate glassware.

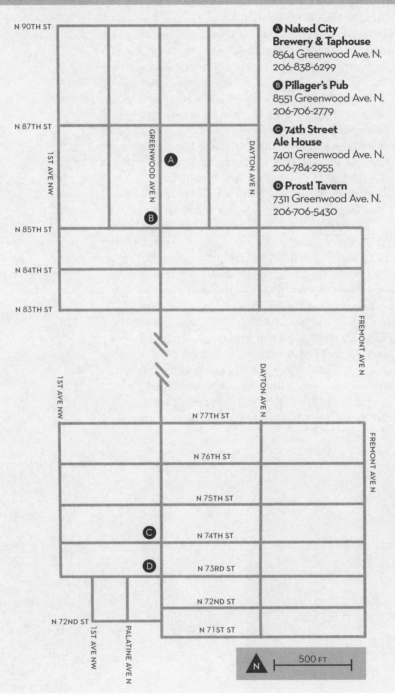

**Ⓐ Naked City
Brewery & Taphouse**
8564 Greenwood Ave. N.
206-838-6299

Ⓑ Pillager's Pub
8551 Greenwood Ave. N.
206-706-2779

**Ⓒ 74th Street
Ale House**
7401 Greenwood Ave. N.
206-784-2955

Ⓓ Prost! Tavern
7311 Greenwood Ave. N.
206-706-5430

On to what might be one of the hidden gems of the Seattle beer scene: the Pub at Piper's Creek. From the outside, it doesn't look like much, and the inside is a match: an unpretentious space with three pool tables, an ever-running jukebox of classic rock favorites, and a kitschy angler theme of nautical bric-a-brac and fishing nets. If you are angling for a good beer, though, the Pub at Piper's Creek is the place to be. With an ever-changing selection and a focus on finding obscure beers, the knowledgeable bartenders pride themselves on helping customers find the perfect pint from among the pub's 15 rotating taps. It's a bit out of the way, but the Pub at Piper's Creek is worth the trip.

DON'T MISS

- The Big Lebrewski Imperial Stout (the beer and the tap handle) at Naked City.

- The pilsner, schwarzbier, or doppelbock at Pillager's Pub (trust me: go with the pilsner if you go for "Das Boot").

- Seeking unusual brews with the passionate staff at Pub at Piper's Creek.

UNIVERSITY DISTRICT

The boisterous Big Time Brewery & Alehouse is the city's original brewpub, housed in a space with big front windows, a bright interior, a large bar, and a back room complete with shuffleboard. It's easy to see why, since 1988, U-Dub students and faculty have come here in droves, to study and socialize over Big Time's wide selection of tasty tipples. Big Time brews a variety of beer styles and and, much to the pleasure of hopheads, there always seems to be at least a couple of IPAs on tap. Very little of the beer makes it outside the brewpub's confines, thanks to fans who drink it as quickly as the brewers can make it. If you're lucky, the very special wheat wine, Old Sol, will be available. Brewed on the Lunar New Year and released on the summer solstice, Old Sol is Big

BIG TIME BREWERY & ALEHOUSE
4133 University Way NE
Seattle, 206-545-4509
bigtimebrewery.com

Brewers squeeze out big beers at Big Time's tiny brewery.

Time's summer barley wine. That's right, a summer barley wine. Old Sol's grain bill is nearly half wheat, and the result is a spicy, creamy, citrusy dessert-in-a-glass beer that is warmer than a summer day. The winter barley wine, Old Woody, is just as wonderful. Produced on a schedule opposite to that of Old Sol, this hop-lovers barley wine is brewed in June and released each year at a more appropriate date for the style, December 1.

If you miss out on the barley and wheat wine, don't fret. There are plenty of other well-made beers to enjoy at Big Time. Old Rip Oatmeal Stout, Prime Time Pale Ale, and Coal Creek Porter are favorites among the locals. The brewers enjoy experimenting with hops, so there usually is something hoppy in the fermenter. Fans of cask beer will enjoy the cask-conditioned brews that Big Time offers, and for the IPA lovers, the cask is often filled with Bhagwan's Best IPA, a highly hopped Northwest-style IPA with loads of grapefruit flavor and aromas.

Another stop in the "U" District (so close to Big Time, you could throw a stein at it from there) is better known for its food, but Shultzy's Sausage ("Seattle's Wurst restaurant since 1989!") offers a nice array of imported German and other European beers and a handful of local craft beers both on draft and in bottles. Just to show how serious they are about the beer at Shultzy's, they hold beer classes once a month that focus on different varieties of beer, what they taste like, and how they are brewed. Too bad it doesn't count toward college credit.

Finally, descend (carefully) into the College Inn Pub by way of a rather steep set of stairs and you immediately feel like you are entering the Dark Ages, complete with obscure lighting, plaster walls, and arguably the best bar ever to grace a space that could double as a dungeon. The drafts are mostly local, with an emphasis on the more unusual brews that are harder to find. The College Inn Pub is a deceptively large space, but it seems to always be packed with students and those well past their formal-education years. Large tables accommodate the bigger groups, while others gather at the bar or pool tables, or in the small room in the back that's perfect for the less rowdy crowd.

DON'T MISS

- Old Sol or Old Woody barley wines at Big Time.
- Shoestring fries and a local IPA or liter of Köstritzer Black Lager at Shultzy's.
- Making the steep descent into the College Inn Pub, feeling like you're going to a super-secret meeting.

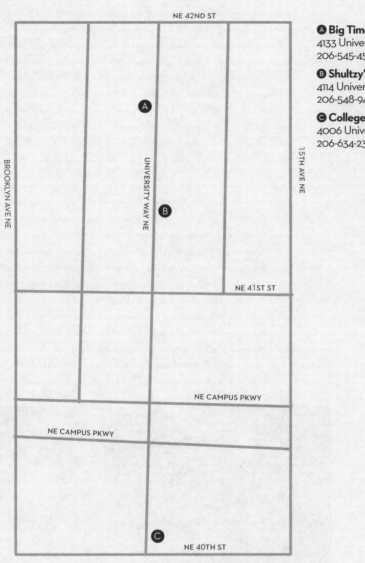

Ⓐ Big Time Brewery
4133 University Way NE
206-545-4509

Ⓑ Shultzy's Sausage
4114 University Way NE
206-548-9461

Ⓒ College Inn Pub
4006 University Way NE
206-634-2307

NE 42ND ST

NE 41ST ST

NE CAMPUS PKWY

NE CAMPUS PKWY

NE 40TH ST

BROOKLYN AVE NE

UNIVERSITY WAY NE

15TH AVE NE

N 100 FT

WEST SEATTLE

You could easily make up your own pub crawl on California Avenue in the swank West Seattle area. You'd work up a bit of a thirst, because the locations are slightly more spread out than on other pub crawls. But isn't that what pub crawls are for?

The first stop would be Porterhouse. A family-friendly gastro-pub with an open and inviting interior and a large patio for beer al fresco, Porterhouse gets rave reviews for its 25 taps, which include ciders, a cask beer, and two beers on nitro. The taps are always changing, and the focus is on West Coast ales, with a few other styles thrown in for specific holidays and just to keep things interesting. There's also a nice selection of craft beer in bottles and cans.

As you make your way down trendy California Avenue, you might want to stop by Seattle's newer Prost! pub. Like its Greenwood Avenue cousin, Prost! West Seattle is a diminutive pub with an all-German draft list. This West Seattle location doesn't offer the number of taps as its older counterpart, but, like the original Prost!, the beers are all served in the proper glassware for the beer style—with 0.3-, 0.5- and 1-liter choices. The Prost! establishments are part of a group of four German-themed locations in Seattle that also include South Lake Union's Feierabend and Die BierStube in the Ravenna neighborhood.

Billing itself as King County's first certified organic brewery, Elliott Bay Brewery Pub is a must-stop location, with its well-balanced selection of hand-crafted beers including an interesting range of IPAs and several Belgian-style beers on draft. Some winners to seek include the No Doubt Stout, Demolition Ale, and Dry-

You pick the samples on the taster tray at Elliott Bay.

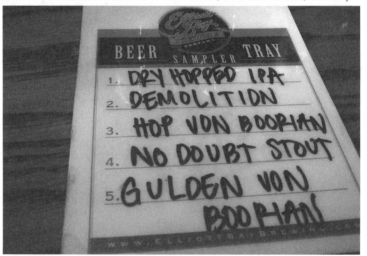

Hopped IPA. Very helpful and knowledgeable servers are quick to get you a sample of any of the beers, or they might suggest the taster tray, which gives you five samples of your choice.

No trip to West Seattle is complete, though, without a visit to Beveridge Place Pub. That is not a misspelling. The pub is named for Beveridge Place, the cross street on which the establishment lies on California Avenue; owners Gary Sink and Terri Griffith couldn't resist the play on words when they renamed their pub a few years ago to better reflect their growing passion for beer. Often voted Washington's best alehouse by *Northwest Brewing News* readers, Beveridge Place is really two different scenes. At the back is a game room—darts, pool, shuffleboard, and sports on TV. The front room feels a lot like a larger rendition of your favorite aunt and uncle's comfortable living room, complete with vintage décor, comfy couches, and board games. They even allow well-behaved dogs inside, and it's not uncommon to see a dog resting beside the table where his or her human is enjoying a beer.

Beveridge Place Pub pours from 25 taps, 15 of which are always rotating—there's something new as soon as the previous keg has blown. One tap is dedicated to rotating Belgian beers such as De-lirium Tremens, Val-Dieu, Chimay, and Celis Grotten. The regular taps focus on Washington's breweries, but the rotating taps will often feature craft beers from Oregon, California, and across the United States. On the left-hand side of the bar, several taps that are separated from the rest of the group feature stronger beers such as barley wines and imperial stouts. It's not uncommon to find a rare beer, such as a vintage barley wine, on tap in that cor-ner. Beveridge Place Pub also has a list of bottled beers, more than 100 items long, featuring some of the best and most unique beers and beer styles from around the world.

Insider tip: there is no kitchen at Bev-eridge Place, so pa-trons are encouraged to order from one of the many neighbor-hood restaurants and bring it in, or bring food from home; just ask for a menu book and start looking for that perfect meal to pair with the beer you just ordered.

ELLIOTT BAY BREWERY PUB
4720 California Ave. SW
Seattle, 206-932-8695
elliottbaybrewing.com/west_seattle

Look to the Dark Side: taps on the far left at Beveridge Place pour dark and strong stuff.

- No Doubt Stout and Dry-Hopped IPA at Elliott Bay.
- The "dark side" of stouts and barley wines on the left side of the bar at Beveridge Place Pub.

SUBURBS

BIG AL BREWING
9832 14th Ave. SW
Seattle, 206-453-4487
bigalbrewing.com

While you wouldn't expect to find in them or any suburbs the bevy of beers that the city proper offers, you can still find artisan beer in the outer limits of Seattle and its environs. Case in point: a business park in the White Center district is an unlikely place to trek to for craft beer, but the folks at Big Al Brewing keep beer fans coming back for more. You never know what they are going to be brewing up next, but clearly they are having fun and want you to have fun with them. Big Al's regular beers are ubiquitous across Seattle, but the tasting room at the brewery is the place to check in on the stuff they're experimenting with—in one visit, you might find a sour ale like those found in Belgium, an Abbey-style wheat beer, and a smoked porter. The tasting room down-stairs invites you to sit, sample, and ask as many questions about the beers as you want, while the upstairs area is akin to a family room, with couches, a large TV, games, and darts.

In Renton, there's a spot in the far corner of the Dog & Pony Alehouse and Grill that is indicative of the relationship owners Jay and Kristen Fisher have with craft brewers. It's called the Wall of Fame. Take a close look, and you will see messages handwritten by some of the region's most respected and creative brewers,

Owner Jay Fisher toasts the Wall of Fame at the Dog & Pony.

who migrate to the Dog & Pony for brewers night, or to just stop in for a brew or two.

Don't be fooled by its lackluster exterior, and don't be thwarted if you can't find a parking spot in the minimal lot. It's best to park on a neigh-borhood side street and hoof it to the Dog & Pony. Inside, you'll find a very cozy, friendly place with a few couches interspersed among tables, and an ample bar on the far end, next to the pool table. The Dog & Pony is full of regulars, but it doesn't take long for the denizens and staff to make you feel like you have been going there for years as you choose a beer from the list of more than 30 taps. Jay Fisher is a former brewer whose love for beer is apparent in his quick smile and in the ever-changing beer list. This is a place that doesn't serve the same beers over and over, and it also doesn't serve the stuff everybody else is pouring. Insider tip: if you want to fit in like a regular, don't ask what's on tap. It's always updated on the large chalkboard menu to the left of the bar.

DON'T MISS

- Sourlicious, a Flanders-style sour ale that has been bourbon-barrel conditioned, at Big Al's, in Seattle's White Center neighborhood.

- Reading the Wall of Fame while sipping your selection from 30-plus taps at the Dog & Pony in Renton.

NORTH PUGET SOUND

There is a certain quality of life in this region that is unique in the state. Despite its close proximity to the big city of Seattle, the pace is a lot more laid-back, and people take time to smile and say hello. Perhaps because of the large artisan population in this region, individuality is encouraged and respected. That renegade spirit carries over to the breweries and pubs that dot this region—from a state-of-the-art brewery that can be controlled through a laptop to an off-the-beaten-path brewpub that doubles as a wedding chapel.

MUKILTEO AND EVERETT

Just north of Seattle, in the bedroom community of Mukilteo, Diamond Knot Brewing Co. has been creating solidly constructed brews since 1994. Founders Bob Maphet and Brian Sollenberger met at the BEEWBC (you know, the Boeing Everett Employees Wine and Beer Club). Both were homebrewers who had let their hobby get "out of control," according to Maphet. Their professional brewing careers started when they sublet a back room of a waterfront pub, Cheers Too, first making beer for that pub and, eventually, a handful of other accounts. The fledgling brewery was definitely a moonlighting job, with both men still working full time at Boeing, brewing on weekends, and distributing in the evenings after work.

Their hard labor paid off, though, and Maphet and Sollenberger

DIAMOND KNOT BREWERY & ALE-HOUSE
621A Front St.
Mukilteo, 425-355-4488
diamondknot.com

(Left) Industrial IPA is a stronger version of Diamond Knot's IPA. (Right) The label for Diamond Knot's Brown Ale depicts the brewery's namesake.

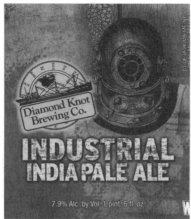 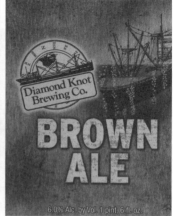

wound up buying Cheers Too—now Diamond Knot Brewery & Alehouse. The name comes from a ship that sank near Port Angeles in 1947; it was full of canned salmon, and in the day, it was thought the cans couldn't be salvaged. The beancounters were ready to write them off as a loss, but a few inventive North Puget Sound–type people utilized what was then an innovative water vacuum and collected most of the tuna cans. The wreckage is considered a prime diving location to this day, and the story serves as a reminder of the power of perseverance. "The shipping people said collecting all those cans could never be done," Maphet says. "When we were opening our brewery, folks said that two people working full time, brewing beer on weekends, and self-distributing? That couldn't get done either. But we did it too." They did it several times over, in fact. In addition to the original location, the brewery has a second brewpub in Mukilteo, Diamond Knot Lincoln Avenue, and a third establishment, Camano Lodge, a pub on Camano Island.

The IPA is Diamond Knot's flagship beer, with the Industrial IPA coming in a close second. It is a stronger version of the regular IPA with 25 percent more grain and double the hops. Brown Ale is another popular selection; Glacier hops, a less common variety, gives the beer a unique, slightly herbal finish.

SCUTTLEBUTT BREWING CO.

1524 W. Marine View Dr. Everett, 425-257-9316 scuttlebuttbrewing.com

In Everett, in the shadow of Boeing, is the Scuttlebutt Brewing Co., started in 1995 by husband and wife team Phil and Cynthia Bannon. The brewery is named after Cynthia, whose father nicknamed her "Scuttlebutt" before she was born—a reference to the pregnancy rumors that were floating around the naval base where the family lived. Cynthia's dad called her that until her thirteenth birthday, when the budding teen asked him to please drop the term of endearment. He followed the spirit of her request, and Cynthia has

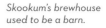

Skookum's brewhouse used to be a barn.

been called simply "Scuttle" by friends and family ever since.

Year-round brews include the award-winning Amber Ale, the brewery's most popular beer; Gale Force, an easy-drinking IPA; and head brewer Matt Stromberg's personal favorite, the ESB served on nitro. Seasonal selections include Tripel 7 Belgian Ale, with hints of pear alongside clove and banana; a strong, malty weizenbock; and 10 Below, an imperial dunkelweiss with a crisp, citrusy aroma and rich, chocolate finish. While the brewery has no retail outlet and is closed to the public, interested tourists can make an appointment for a tour. Best bet is to go to the small Scuttlebutt pub, which is located several blocks away on Everett's waterfront.

DON'T MISS

- Diamond Knot's bold, bright Industrial IPA.
- Scuttlebutt's ESB poured from a nitro tap, a smooth, easy-drinker.

ARLINGTON TO BELLINGHAM

North of Everett, the landscape becomes decidedly more rural—but it is still surprising to find a brewery on a horse ranch. That is where you will find Skookum Brewery, a stone's throw off some dusty country roads in Arlington. Skookum is what happens when a family gets bitten by the brewing bug. After years in the construction business, husband and wife owners Ron Wachter and Jackie Jenkins built their home on the acreage, repurposing a 1918 dairy barn that had been scheduled to be torn down

SKOOKUM BREWERY
19529 17th Dr. NE
Arlington, 360-652-4917
skookumbrewing.com

in neighboring Marysville into their new home. The couple got permission to disassemble the barn, and stored it for a couple of years until the right property came along. Part of the building that houses the brewery, which is also a former barn, was built from those materials as well.

Skookum is a production brewery but holds tasting-room hours on Friday evenings and Saturday afternoons. That is when Wachter and Jenkins open up their home, literally, to the public. It is mostly a local crowd that gathers under umbrella-covered tables to catch up and sip from the nine or so beers that are usually on tap. Jackass IPA, a solid beer in the Northwest style; and Amber's Hot Friend, a hopped-up amber-style beer, are the best-sellers, but the beers nearly take backstage to the brewery's setting. After all, it's not every day you get to sip on a craft beer with horses whinnying in the nearby pasture and dogs frolicking at your feet.

In Anacortes, the Boeing Co. has played a role in another brewpub's beginnings. Like Diamond Knot's owners, Rockfish Grill and Anacortes Brewery co-founder Allen Rhoades also was a Boeing employee and moonlighted in the brewery for years before deciding to devote his time fully to its operations. The brewery produces more than 20 styles of beer, so there is bound to be something for everyone. Top sellers at the brewpub are the crisp, refreshing pilsner, a Czech-style lager with a smooth finish, the IPA, and the porter.

Insider tip: if you plan on traveling from Anacortes to Bellingham, or vice versa, instead of connecting with Interstate 5, take the scenic Chuckanut Drive (Route 11; chuckanutdrive.com), which winds along the Samish Bay and through the tiny towns of Allen and Bow. Slow down even more and make a side trip to historic Edison, all 0.6 square miles of it.

For its size, the scenic little city of Bellingham boasts an impressive number of good beer destinations, including two award-winning brewpubs. Boundary Bay Brewery & Bistro, Bellingham's first brewpub, is usually packed, and it's not uncommon to see people waving from table to table at each other or walking up to chat with another group as they sip Inside Passage Ale, a finely crafted IPA, or Old Bounder, Boundary Bay's barley wine. But to really get the locals' treatment at Boundary Bay, head outside and down the stairs to the beer garden, a large expanse of lawn with covered tents, long tables for large groups, a music stage, and a bar with several Boundary Bay taps. Add to it the lush, colorful landscaping and festive outdoor lights and you might mistakenly think you are at a really cool wedding reception—one with great beer.

In addition to the IPA and Old Bounder, some other brews to try

ROCKFISH GRILL, ANACORTES BREWERY
320 Commercial Ave.
Anacortes, 360-588-1720
anacortesrockfish.com

BOUNDARY BAY BREWERY & BISTRO
1107 Railroad Ave.
Bellingham, 360-647-5593
bbaybrewery.com

at Boundary Bay include the highly anticipated winter seasonal, Cabin Fever; the ESB; and the Imperial IPA, the latter of which has finished in both first and second place in different years at the Alpha King Challenge, a national competition held in Denver during the Great American Beer Festival to find the best balanced yet still hoppiest beer in the country.

Speaking of medals, Chuckanut Brewery & Kitchen was just a year old when it earned two gold medals (in the European-style dunkel and Vienna-style lager categories) and two silver medals (in the German-style schwarzbier and German-style pilsner categories) at its first Great American Beer Festival. The beers impressed the judges so much, they also gave Chuckanut the title of Small Brewpub of the Year in 2009.

Chuckanut's owner and brewmaster Will Kemper has been a fixture in the craft beer industry for years, working mostly as a consultant for startup craft breweries, engineering and supervising the construction and brewery setup, creating the recipes, and, finally, training the brewer to take over production. Kemper has

CHUCKANUT BREWERY & KITCHEN
601 W. Holly St.
Bellingham, 360-752-3377
chuckanutbreweryand-kitchen.com

Mari and Will Kemper traveled extensively when Will consulted for breweries.

a degree in chemical engineering and holds several diplomas from different brewing schools; he even taught brewery engineering for the American Brewers Guild in Davis, Calif., for several years in the 1990s. So, when Kemper was ready to launch his dream brewery, he poured all his experience, contacts, and background as a consultant, engineer, and brewer into Chuckanut, with the objective of bringing state-of-the-art technology typically reserved for large, industrial breweries to the artistic elements of a small craft brew house.

Thanks to the relationships he developed as a consultant, Kemper was able to work with Canada-based DME Brewing Services, which specializes in building brewing equipment for craft breweries, to invent special equipment for Chuckanut. The entire brewery is run by a computer system that allows the brewers to dial in temperatures and other specifications in the brewing process to the exact decimal. The same system is run via satellite, so brewers can control functions on any computer, even a laptop at home.

Chuckanut, which is named after the indigenous Native Americans of the area, specializes in German-style beers but also features a handful of ales popular in the Northwest, such as a pale ales and a porter. The beers are not filtered yet are clear as a bell; the brewing process allows time for any sediment to settle in each beer before it moves on to the next stage, resulting in a gorgeous, clean brew.

Chuckanut is an ideal starting point for a five-stop pub crawl in the heart of Bellingham. From there head to Uisce, an Irish pub with a nice selection of Irish and British beers on tap. Continue walking and you'll find the Copper Hog, a gastropub with about 20 taps, all well selected and ever-changing. Close by is Boundary Bay, and from there it is a short walk to the Green Frog Café Acoustic Tavern, a great pub with live music, guitars hanging on the wall for impromptu jam sessions, and a very intelligently selected rotating tap list.

A Chuckanut Brewery & Kitchen
601 W. Holly St.
360-752-3377

B Uisce Irish Pub
1319 Commercial St.
360-738-7939

C The Copper Hog
1327 N. State St.
360-927-7888

D Boundary Bay
1107 Railroad Ave.
360-647-5593

E Green Frog Café
902 N. State St.
360-756-1213

North Fork is a scrappy little brewpub with a lot going on inside.

NORTH FORK BREWERY
6186 Mount Baker Hwy.
Deming, 360-599-2337
northforkbrewery.com

A short drive east of Bellingham is a brewpub that some might consider to be the polar opposite of Chuckanut. Not that the folks at North Fork Brewery don't take their beer seriously; they just do so in a very different way. Where Chuckanut's brewery is state-of-the art, North Fork's is scrappy, built on the fly with materials on hand. Chuckanut's brewery feels like every inch was planned for efficiency. North Fork's brewery has expanded organically through the years. Yet, there are similarities, too: Kemper has his diplomas and degrees, and North Fork owner Sandy Savage has the bragging rights of being the first homebrewer to attend and graduate from the Siebel Institute of Technology, a highly respected brewing school in both Chicago and outside of Munich, Germany.

North Fork Brewery calls itself a beer shrine, pizzeria, and wedding chapel, but it is a whole lot more. Savage, who was the brewer at Triple Rock Brewery and Alehouse in Berkeley, Calif., in the 1980s, and his wife, Vicki, a hospital manager, knew they wanted to have their own brewpub some day. The pathway to that day came when they came across an abandoned pizzeria on the Mount Baker Highway. The couple picked up and moved from Berkeley into the 100-year-old building in Deming that was to one day be their dream brewpub. They continued to live there for more than a dozen years while they built the brewery and designed the pub themselves. One of the toughest things about moving was finding space for the beer-related stuff that Sandy collected, each time with a promise that "it will go great in the brewpub." He was right. Ask an employee where the beer shrine is at North Fork, and you will be told you are standing in it. Nearly every inch of the place is covered with beer signs, trays, old bottles, and other breweriana—more than 90 years of beer covered in all.

The wedding chapel is for real, too. Vicki, an ordained minister, has married more than 100 couples in the corner of the brewpub in front of the pretty stained glass piece right by the front door. But don't think you can have an impromptu nuptial service at the North Fork. It takes some planning. First you have to move the table that normally occupies that corner. Then the rug gets moved into place, and the bar becomes a pizza buffet for the reception. It's definitely not something you can perform during regular business hours. "We do weddings in the mornings, before we open," Vicki says.

With so many quirks, it shouldn't be surprising that barley wine, not one of your more popular styles, is among North Fork's best-selling beers. One or the other of the brewery's two barley wines—either Hair of the Frog, smooth and rich in flavors of plums and dark fruit mingled with citrusy hops, or Spotted Owl, a sweeter barley wine with hints of raisins and cherries—is always on tap at North Fork. Each is brewed just once a year. When one runs out, the other goes on the tap, and the one that runs out is brewed again, allowing for about six months of aging. Because the barley wine continues to age while it is being poured, regulars get to taste how the beer evolves, making for a continual "vertical tasting."

DON'T MISS

- Sipping your choice of beers "in the tasting room" (i.e., under the tree canopy) at Skookum Brewery (please call ahead to plan your visit).

- Boundary Bay Imperial IPA in the beer garden on a warm summer day.

- Chuckanut's well-designed beers, especially the German-style brews. The kölsch is as close to Cologne, Germany, the style's birthplace, as you can get in the United States.

- Whichever barley wine is currently on tap at North Fork, complete with a tour of the beer shrine. Wedding optional.

PUGET SOUND PENINSULAS

**SILVER CITY
BREWING CO.**

2799 NW Myhre Rd.
Silverdale, 360-698-5879
silvercitybrewery.com

The city of Silverdale, located on the Kitsap Peninsula, boasts as its claim to fame Kitsap Mall, the largest shopping mall between Seattle-Tacoma and the Pacific Ocean. It really should brag that it is home to an award-winning brewpub, Silver City Brewing, which has been making excellent beer since 1996. The expansive, two-story brewpub has a bar area with some pub tables, plus restaurant seating that stretches back into a second room, and a smaller area upstairs that feels more like an intimate pub. Despite

(Left) Silver City's Fat Scotch Ale is a multiple Great American Beer Festival gold medalist. (Right) Ridgetop Red is a very approachable Irish-style red ale from Silver City.

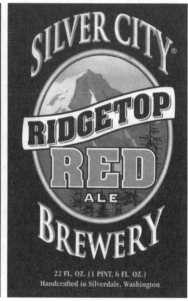

all the space, the vibrant brewpub always fills up, and there's often a waiting list to be seated in the restaurant. You might even find yourself elbow-to-elbow with happy beer drinkers at the bar.

The reason for Silver City's popularity? Consistently award-winning beers. Brewmaster Don Spencer and his team brew a half-dozen year-round beers, and nearly 20 seasonals, which means something different is always on tap. Of the year-round beers, try the Fat Scotch Ale, brewed with a touch of peat malt for a whisky-like character, or the Indianola Pale Ale, the brewery's IPA with loads of hops in both aroma and flavor. The wide range of seasonal beers showcases the depth of talent in this brewery, from the Czech-inspired Gold Mountain Pilsner to the rich, fruity Old Scrooge Christmas Ale, both multiple award-winners at the Great American Beer Festival.

Two seaports on the Olympic Peninsula do not disappoint for craft beer. The first, picturesque Port Townsend, is home to Port

Townsend Brewing Co., the second brewery to adopt the name: the first was established in 1906 and closed during Prohibition. Like its predecessor, the second version of Port Townsend Brewing Co. is still is a production brewery, although the space does have two small tasting rooms, which get crowded quickly as locals get off work. When the weather is nice, the outdoor beer garden is the place to be, with a grassy lawn, lots of chairs, and tables with colorful umbrellas. Some beers to try: the twice dry-hopped Hop Diggity IPA; the stout, reminiscent of bitter chocolate; and the Boatyard Bitter, a nicely balanced English-style bitter.

Over in the other "port" town, Port Angeles, Ed and Wanda Smith call their brewpub "The Friendly Place," and—true enough—it doesn't take long for a complete stranger to feel right at home at Peaks. The couple has owned the restaurant and bar since 1999; in 2005, they added a tiny two-barrel brewing system. It's small, but the brewery cranks out a lot of beer under Ed's direction. In addition to its evolving lineup of house beers, Peaks Brewpub also offers an impressive number of guest taps that are always changing. Ed's passion for beer is contagious, and he is quite adept at sniffing out unusual brews for his guest taps, making Peaks the perfect place to park yourself with a pint in Port Angeles.

PORT TOWNSEND BREWING CO.
330 Tenth St., Port Townsend, 360-385-9967
porttownsendbrewing.com

PEAKS
130 S. Lincoln St.
Port Angeles
360-452-2802
peakspub.com

DON'T MISS

- Fat Scotch Ale, Indianola Pale Ale, Whoop Pass Double IPA, or Gold Mountain Pilsner at Silver City.
- Hop Diggity IPA or Strait Stout at Port Townsend Brewing.
- Wanda Fuca Gold, Train Wreck IPA, or anything Peaks is doing with plums at the time. Don't question; just ask for a taster.

SOUTH SOUND TO OREGON

With Seattle so close by, Tacoma and Olympia often get overlooked, but both cities enjoy a thriving craft beer culture.

TACOMA

Several great beer establishments call Tacoma home. The city's old Heidelberg Brewery sits directly behind Harmon Brewing Co.'s brewery and restaurant, making for an interesting juxtaposition of Tacoma's brewing history. Harmon usually has eight of its beers on tap at its prime location in the city's university and museum district—a selection of standards plus a few seasonals. Point Defiance IPA, the first beer commercially brewed by Harmon in 1997, remains the most popular of the brewery's five year-round

HARMON BREWING CO.
1938 Pacific Ave. S.
Tacoma, 253-383-2739
harmonbrewingco.com

HARMON TAPROOM
204 St. Helens Ave.
Tacoma, 253-212-2725
harmonbrewingco.com

ENGINE HOUSE NO. 9
611 N. Pine St., Tacoma
253-272-3435
ehouse9.com

offerings. Harmon also owns a neighborhood pub in Tacoma called the Hub, where Harmon beers are poured. The Harmon Taproom, a second 15-barrel production brewery with connected taproom, opened in 2010, giving this expanding brewery a chance to market its beers beyond Tacoma.

Engine House No. 9 is worth a visit for the venue alone. This brewpub is housed in an old fire station, built in 1907 and placed on the National Register of Historic Places in 1975. As would be expected, the décor speaks to the building's rich history, with photos of firefighters and other fire-related memorabilia on the walls. E-9, as it is called, features eight of its own beers on tap, plus a variety of guest taps, including three cask-conditioned ales.

The Parkway Tavern has been a neighborhood pub for decades, and the proof is on the walls, where you can look at historic photos of the establishment in its many iterations. The pub itself is

The "E-9" is located in a historic firehouse.

really more like two separate establishments. The front room features an ample bar and several large tables, giving it a real public house atmosphere. The back half of the building has a game room with pinball, darts, and other pub games, plus a smaller room for more intimate gatherings. The service staff at the Parkway is extremely informative and friendly. You can tell the servers were hired because they love to talk about beer and are excited about introducing new beers to willing customers. Under its latest ownership, the Parkway has expanded to more than 30 taps, most of which see a different craft beer every time a new keg is tapped. The Parkway likes to showcase smaller Washington breweries but also will reach into other states.

The high tin roof and South African mahogany bar of the Swiss Tavern, built in 1913 as a gathering place for the Swiss Society, still speak of another era. The current version of The Swiss opened in 1993, one of the first attempts to revive a part of Tacoma that had fallen into disrepair. Now the district, which is close to the University of Washington's Tacoma campus and the Tacoma Art Museum, is thriving. Military men and women stationed in neighboring Joint Base Lewis-McChord have been going to The Swiss for years, and many have sent over photos or brought back military memorabilia with the words "I'd rather be at The Swiss" on them. You'll find the tributes to their favorite hangout, homages to happier days, all over the walls at The Swiss—along with the accordion collection of Dale Chihuly, the world-renowned glass artist who grew up in Tacoma. Several pieces of Chihuly glass are also on display here, on permanent loan to The Swiss and perfectly lit for all to enjoy. It's the only pub in the world decorated with more than $300,000 of Chihuly artwork.

"I'D RATHER BE AT THE SWISS"

When you walk up to the bar at The Swiss in Tacoma, be sure to look above the taps. You'll see an American flag backing a photo of a young soldier and two of his comrades; the soldier is smiling into the camera and holding a make-shift sign that reads "I'd rather be at The Swiss." But this man's image does not join his military sisters and brothers on the busy walls. It sits alone in a place of honor at the center of the bar, the heart of the pub. The man in the photo is Pat Tillman, the former Arizona Cardinals football player who put his NFL career on hold to serve his country in the after-math of the terrorist attacks on September 11, 2001.

The photo is the last known picture taken of Tillman, who was based in Fort Lewis before he was deployed to Afghani-stan. It was given to The Swiss by Tillman's family shortly after he was killed in 2004. In respect to the family, The Swiss requests that no photographs be taken of the photo, but countless people have come to pay their respects to Tillman.

Walls at The Swiss are covered with messages from soldiers.

DON'T MISS

- Point Defiance IPA is a real winner, but Harmon's seasonal beers are usually a good bet, too.

- With three tap handles, try what's on cask at Engine House No. 9.

- Drink in the history while drinking your choice of beer from the number of smaller Washington breweries showcased at the Parkway Tavern.

- Grab a beer of your choice at The Swiss and peruse the collections: the Chihuly glass pieces over the bar, his accordions, and the military tributes.

OLYMPIA TO OREGON BORDER

Fish Brewing Co. got its start early in the microbrew movement, in 1993, in downtown Olympia, Washington's capital city. Fish's first brewery was made mostly of old dairy equipment, a common practice at the time because small systems for craft breweries were not yet being manufactured. The original brewery was located where the Fish Tale Brew Pub is today; the brewery expanded and moved directly across the street in 1996. It began bottling a year later, allowing Fish to expand well beyond the Puget Sound market.

Fish is a certified organic brewery with six year-round beers that are available throughout the Northwest: Amber, IPA, Wild Salmon Pale Ale, Blonde, Mud Shark Porter, and Trout Stout. Seasonal beers include Winterfish, a full-bodied brew with a touch of alcohol warmth and a nice hoppy balance. In addition to its original brand, Fish also owns and brews the Leavenworth Biers brand of German-style beers, which was founded in the Bavarian-themed town of Leavenworth, Wash. Some Leavenworth beers to

FISH TALE BREW PUB, FISH BREWING CO.
515 Jefferson St. SE
Olympia, 360-943-3650
fishbrewing.com

(Left) Fish Brewing's beers are certified organic. (Right) Leavenworth's German-inspired beers are brewed at the Fish brewery.

look for include the Boulder Bend Dunkelweizen, a rich, cloudy-brown beer with hints of lemon and chocolate, and the Eight Mile Alt, a medium-bodied brew that strikes a nice balance between malt and hops.

Fish also owns Spire Mountain Draft Ciders, which distributes both draft and bottled versions of its pear cider, regular apple cider, and the specialty Dark and Dry Apple Cider, a tart cider that is balanced by additions of molasses and brown sugar. Spire Mountain's cidery occupies its own space in the Fish brewery.

And now south to Centralia, where Dick Young (owner of Northwest Sausage & Deli, a popular Centralia restaurant and meat counter with house-made sausages and smoked meats) caught the homebrewing bug in 1984. Young was selling homebrew supplies at the deli when he decided to go pro and set up a brewery onsite at the restaurant in 1990. Dick's Brewing Co. has since expanded to a larger onsite production brewery with more than

DICK'S BREWING CO.
3516 Galvin Rd.
Centralia, 800-586-7760
dicksbeer.com

Dick Young is immortalized on the label of Dick's Double Diamond Winter Ale.

20 different craft beer varieties. Patrons of the deli can enjoy a Dick's beer along with sandwiches created from the house-smoked meats. They can also select bottles to go from a large cooler at the meat counter.

Dick's Barley Wine, a lightly hopped version with loads of caramel and touches of raisin in both aroma and flavor, is a beer to seek, as is Dick's Belgian Tripel Style Ale, a dangerously drinkable beer that presents flavors of tropical fruit and a smooth, creamy finish. The brewery's flagship beer, Dick's Danger Ale, was Young's favorite. Young passed away in 2009, but his memory lives on in Dick's Double Diamond Winter Ale, a warming seasonal brew that artfully combines bready and caramel aromas with a generous dose of hops to cut the sweetness. It is a fitting tribute to this craft beer pioneer.

An easy pub crawl will take you through the state capital's eclectic downtown. Starting at the Fish Tale Brew Pub, it is a short walk to the Eastside Club Tavern, a not-to-miss beer drinker's paradise with more than 35 taps, some on nitro. Further on is 4th Avenue Ale House, a local pub with a good selection of rotating taps. End your crawl, whatever the time, at the Spar Café, a McMenamins brewpub that serves breakfast, lunch, and dinner along with brews made in-house.

SPAR CAFÉ
114 Fourth Ave. E.
Olympia, 360-357-6444
mcmenamins.com

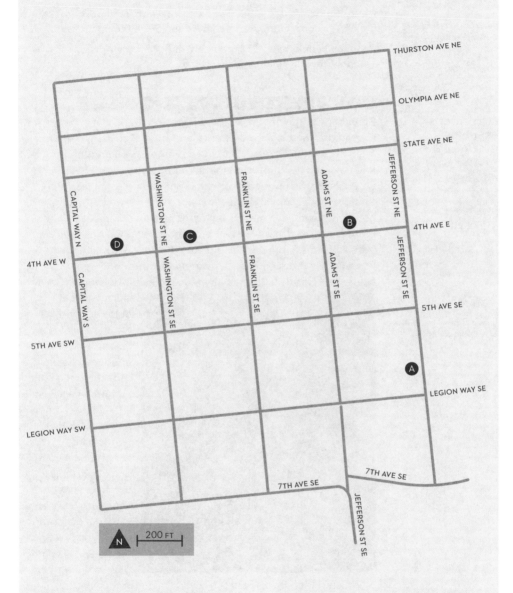

THURSTON AVE NE

OLYMPIA AVE NE

STATE AVE NE

4TH AVE E

4TH AVE W

5TH AVE SE

5TH AVE SW

LEGION WAY SE

LEGION WAY SW

7TH AVE SE

7TH AVE SE

CAPITAL WAY N

CAPITAL WAY S

WASHINGTON ST NE

WASHINGTON ST SE

FRANKLIN ST NE

FRANKLIN ST SE

ADAMS ST NE

ADAMS ST SE

JEFFERSON ST NE

JEFFERSON ST SE

JEFFERSON ST SE

N 200 FT

Ⓐ **Fish Tale Brew Pub**
515 Jefferson St. SE
360-943-3650

Ⓑ **Eastside Club Tavern**
410 Fourth Ave. E.
360-357-9985

Ⓒ **4th Avenue Ale House**
210 Fourth Ave. E.
360-786-1444

Ⓓ **Spar Café**
114 Fourth Ave. E.
360-357-6444

- Try the seasonals at the Fish Tale Brew Pub, or choose from the Leavenworth German-style beers and Spire Mountain Ciders.

- Enjoy your choice of Dick's beers either on draft or from the cooler over a handmade sandwich.

COLUMBIA RIVER GORGE

**EVERYBODY'S
BREWING**
151 E. Jewett Blvd.
White Salmon, 509-637-2774
everybodysbrewing.com

Everybody's Brewing in White Salmon, Wash., is just across the river and a short ride away from Hood River, Ore., home of three other brewpubs. Owners Doug Ellenberger and Christine McAleer have created a stunning environment at Everybody's Brewing, with a large, family-oriented restaurant area and a sizeable deck that provides some of the most spectacular views in the entire gorge. Sixteen beers are on tap at all times, with about half of them made onsite in Ellenberger's brewery, which he procured from a Japanese brewery, complete with Japanese instructions. Everybody's Brewing makes a variety of year-round and seasonal beers. The Oatmeal Stout is a winner, as is the Hoedown Brown

Doug Ellenberger toasts the great view at Everybody's Brewing with one of his popular brews.

Ale, a very quaffable beer with a low enough alcohol content to warrant ordering another. The other taps pour a rotating selection of beers from other breweries; Ellenberger used to work for Portland's Point Blank Distributing, which focuses on craft beers, so you know the guest taps at Everybody's Brewing are always going to be worth a try.

Walking Man Brewery is the "living room" of Stevenson, a gathering place not just for its residents but also its visitors. In the winter months, that living room is pretty small, just a pint-sized brewpub that serves good food and a wide selection of Walking Man's reliably award-winning beers. During the warmer months, though, the living room expands, sprawling out across the outdoor beer garden, where beer fans sit among climbing hop

bines, enjoying local music and exceptional brews. You really can't go wrong with any selection of whatever is on tap—the beers are all good at Walking Man. Most are named with a pedestrian theme: Flip-Flop Pilsner, Homo Erectus IPA, Foot Fetish Brown Ale, Street Walker Malt Liquor. One exception to the walking nomenclature is the Legacy Project beer. Once a year, owner Bob Craig turns over his brewery to work with brewers currently receiving aid from the Glen Hay Falconer Foundation, a nonprofit that provides scholarships

for Northwest brewers to better their craft by attending brewing school. All proceeds from the beer that is created and sold each year go directly to the Foundation.

(Above) Taps at Walking Man with the brewery's familiar logo, the pedestrian street sign. (Below) Glen Hay Falconer's brother, Quentin, center, with Walking Man brewers at a Legacy Foundation beer release celebration.

WALKING MAN BREWING CO.
240 SW First St.
Stevenson, 509-427-5520
walkingmanbrewing.com

DON'T MISS

- The view from the windows, or on a nice day, from the deck, plus Cash Stout Oatmeal Stout, Daily Bread Common Ale, or Country Boy IPA at Everybody's Brewing.

- Street Walker Malt Liquor, Somnambulator Doppelbock, Jaywalker Russian Imperial Stout—really, there isn't a bad one in the bunch at Walking Man Brewing.

CENTRAL AND EASTERN WASHINGTON

Thanks to a smaller population base and a lot of land between towns, this region doesn't get nearly the respect it deserves for its craft beer culture. In fact, the Yakima Valley produces about 75 percent of the hops grown in the United States, according to the Hop Growers of America. Three distinct growing regions, no more than 50 miles (80 km) apart, comprise the valley. Because of its slightly warmer climate, hop growers in the Lower Yakima Valley are able to produce commercially viable amounts of hops from first-year plants (most hop plants need up to three years to reach maturity). The center region, the Yakama Indian Reservation, is known for a climate that is amenable to producing hops with high bittering properties. And the northernmost Moxee Valley, with a slightly cooler climate, is better known for producing the hops used to impart aroma in beer, a property highly prized by home-brewers and craft brewers alike.

The region is also the birthplace of the modern-day brew-pub. It's where Bert Grant built a pub for dining attached to his brewery, so people could enjoy great food with his beers. Brilliant. The brewers of the area today still share Grant's pioneering spirit. There are a lot of great places to find good beer here, if you know where to look.

SPOKANE

I have lived in the Pacific Northwest for long enough to know better, but until I started researching this book, I was not familiar with Spokane's vibrant and growing craft beer culture.

STEAM PLANT GRILL
159 S. Lincoln, Spokane
509-777-3900
steamplantgrill.com

It snows a lot more in Lilac City (as Spokane is sometimes called) than it does in the western half of the state's coastal, more temperate climate. But snow's not a problem in downtown Spokane—that is, it wasn't until 1986: that's when the massive steam plant that provided heat and electricity to most of the downtown area was shut down. Until then, all the pipes providing the heat ran under the sidewalks to various buildings. Those pipes were warm enough to melt the snow, keeping the city's downtown walkways clear for more than 70 years. The landmark building with its twin smokestacks sat idle for almost a decade before finding its new purpose of housing the Steam Plant Grill. The owner's an architect, and attention to detail shows in every corner of this brewpub. It's obvious that extreme care was taken to preserve the integrity of the structure, making for a unique brewpub setting. Eighty-foot ceilings, criss-crossed by catwalks, elevate the scene;

BEER PIONEER: BERT GRANT

It took a crusty Scot from Canada to change the way Americans think about and drink beer. Born in Scotland but raised in Canada, Grant worked as a brewery consultant for years before he opened his trailblazing microbrewery and brewpub. Grant's Yakima Brewing & Malting Co. was among the first microbreweries in the country, and Grant's Brewery Pub, which opened in Yakima, Wash., in 1982, is considered to be the first U.S. brewpub since Prohibition.

Grant's admiration for hops was cultivated in Yakima, where he landed in the late 1960s to build and operate hop-processing plants. His beers were brewed with what, at the time, were considered to be obscene amounts of hops, prompting many to consider him the forefather of the hoppy, Northwest-style IPA. Grant's practice of carrying a vial of hop oil with him to liven up mass-produced domestic beers is legendary. At one point, Grant, knowing that his beers were packed with nutrients, had them analyzed at a lab and listed their vitamin and mineral content on the packaging, much like current food labels; the action prompted a run-in with federal officials, who eventually put a stop to it. Although he died in 2001, Grant's pioneering spirit lives on, in craft breweries across the Pacific Northwest and beyond.

small nooks and crannies call out for private gatherings; and pipes and dials greet you at every turn. One especially intimate room (staff calls it the "proposal room") has a porthole on one end, where the coal was fed in, and pipes covering the walls; it almost feels as if you are sitting inside a pipe organ. Or a steam plant.

While five of the brewpub's 11 beers are brewed in-house on the small system, most are brewed in Idaho by Coeur d'Alene Brewing Co., which is owned by the same group of partners. The Huckleberry Ale, subtle on the berry flavor with a nice, crisp finish; the Lakeside British Ale, a richly flavored nut brown with a nimble body that makes the beer quite drinkable; the Rockford Bay IPA, with a Northwest hop finish that isn't too in-your-face; and the Pullman Porter, a chocolaty offering with enough roast in it to keep things from getting too sweet were standout beers. The best bet is to share a sampler tray with a friend. Five-ounce samples of all 11 beers are arranged by number on a piece of

wood that has been shaped to resemble the Steam Plant's twin
smokestacks. It is one of the better values for a sampler tray that
I have encountered.

Several spots are within walking distance of Steam Plant. Blue
Spark offers beer-knowledgeable servers and always something
unique on its 32 taps. Post Street Ale House has 20 rotating beers
on tap in a large, airy pub. Baby Bar, an aptly named speck of a
bar that shares space with the Neato Burrito restaurant, offers an
equally small yet always well-selected number of taps. For a round
of pool and a nice selection of craft beer, head for Far
West Billiards.

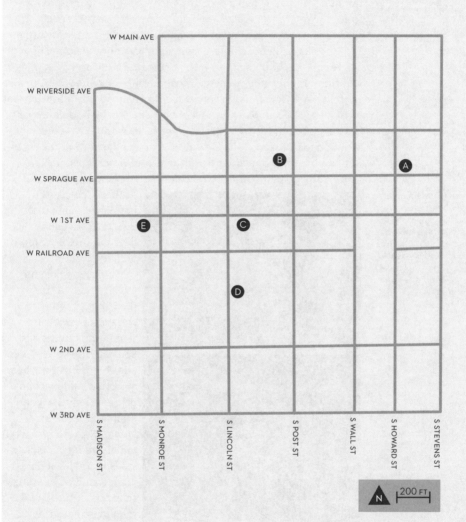

W MAIN AVE

W RIVERSIDE AVE

Ⓑ Ⓐ

W SPRAGUE AVE

W 1ST AVE Ⓔ Ⓒ

W RAILROAD AVE

Ⓓ

W 2ND AVE

W 3RD AVE

S MADISON ST

S MONROE ST

S LINCOLN ST

S POST ST

S WALL ST

S HOWARD ST

S STEVENS ST

N 200 FT

Ⓐ **Blue Spark**
15 S. Howard St.
509-838-5787

Ⓑ **Post Street
Ale House**
1 N. Post St.
509-789-6900

Ⓒ **Baby Bar**
827 W. First Ave.
509-847-1234

Ⓓ **Steam
Plant Grill**
159 S. Lincoln
509-777-3900

Ⓔ **Far West
Billiards**
1001 W. First Ave.
509-455-3429

NORTHERN LIGHTS BREWING CO.

1003 E. Trent Ave.
Spokane, 509-242-2739
northernlightsbrewing.com

A second Spokane brewpub, Northern Lights Brewing Co., is situated at the far end of a small mall, right next to Dry Fly Distilling, a craft spirits distiller of vodka, gin, and whiskey, making for an interesting one-two side trip. Northern Lights was a production brewery for several years before moving into this space, which used to be the Bayou Brewpub, and though the Northern Lights folks have been here for several years now, vestiges of the former resident, such as a New Orleans mural and French Quarter wrought iron, remain. Those trappings, paired with the high-voltage Northern Lights neon sign, make for a slightly surreal entryway. The sampler tray is a good value for the huge number of beers offered. Northern Lights' big seller is the IPA; it has five additions of Cluster, Palisade, and Cascade hops during the brew and is then dry-hopped with Palisades and Amarillo hops. The quite unusual Blueberry Crème balances sweet malt with a fruity tartness: nearly 400 pounds of blueberries are added to each batch at the beginning of fermentation.

(Above) Northern Lights' bottled beers are available throughout the state, but the brewpub offers beers that can't be found in bottles. (Below) Several tap stations like this one dot the lengthy bar at the Viking.

A visit to Spokane must include a trip to the Viking Tavern, the one craft beer location in the city that is consistently voted "best beer bar" and "best beer selection" in local annual competitions. As you approach the Viking, you might wonder if you are at the right place; it looks more like a double-wide trailer on steroids than a beer bar. But the signs reassure you that you have, indeed, arrived. The interior still looks like the inside of a double-wide (complete with fake wood paneling), but the taps reveal the Viking's true calling as a purveyor of fine craft beer. Munch on a free bowl of popcorn while making your selection from 34 taps of rotating beers, or tour the world via the more than 100 bottles from Belgium to Italy, from India to Croatia, plus a dozen or so craft beers from across the United States.

The Elk Public House is a lively tap house situated in what used to be the neighborhood drug store. The interior's focal point, running half the length of the stand-alone brick building, is a copper-sheathed bar. It's easy to imagine that bar's once being an old-fashioned soda fountain, and there's still a neighborhood feel to the place—only now, the neighborhood's bigger: people come from all over Spokane to enjoy a bite and a selection from the pub's nearly 20 rotating taps.

DON'T MISS

- The sampler tray of all the beers at the Steam Plant Grill—5 ounces of all 11 beers. Find a friend to share it with or call a cab to get home.

- The IPA, Chocolate Dunkel, Dark Doppel, and, for fruit beer fans, the unusual Blueberry Crème at Northern Lights.

- Making your way through a bowl of popcorn and the beer of your choice from the extensive draft and bottle list at the Viking.

WINTHROP AND COLVILLE

Entering Winthrop is like walking onto the set of a Spaghetti Western; all the town's buildings look like they were built in the days of the American Old West. The town's theme inspired both the name and look of the Old Schoolhouse Brewery. In its previous life, the building that houses it was a western-wear store, but it was redesigned to look like an old schoolhouse, down to a real bell in the bell tower.

Old Schoolhouse Brewery is a family affair. The interior is cozy and elongated, with a half-wall dividing the bar area from the family-friendly restaurant side. A large patio in the back of the building beckons locals and tourists on warm summer days and evenings. Owners Laura and Casey Ruud bought the brewpub in 2006; their son Blaze does most of the brewing, with Casey assisting. Blaze, who had been working as a physicist before his father asked him to join the family business, takes a scientific approach to the beers at Old Schoolhouse, learning as much as he can and experimenting a bit with seasonals. Blaze's wife, Stephanie, works with the kitchen staff to promote craft beer by cooking with beer and making pairing suggestions on the menu. She also makes sure the servers are educated in their beer styles so they

OLD SCHOOLHOUSE BREWERY
155 Riverside Ave.
Winthrop, 509-996-3183
oldschoolhousebrewery.com

(Top) Old Schoolhouse Brewery inhabits what used to be a western-wear shop. (Below, left) The recipe for the pale ale came to Casey Ruud while jogging. (Below, right) Ruud Awakening, the house favorite, is a well-balanced IPA.

can help fledgling beer fans find the right beer. "We're not bartenders," says Stephanie. "We're beer-fitters."

Ruud Awakening IPA is the house favorite, a nicely balanced IPA that still exhibits a bracing hop profile. Malt mavens will appreciate the Hooligan Stout, a silky smooth creamy brew that is extremely easy to drink. The Rendezvous Porter has aromas of chocolate and citrusy hops with a roasty finish. The Imperial IPA is like a candy bar in a glass: toffee and caramel notes take precedence at the beginning of the sip but give way to a wallop of hops that keeps everything nicely in balance.

LOST FALLS BREWING CO.
347 W. Second St.
Colville, 509-684-0638

Colville is an unlikely location to have deep craft beer roots. But this small city in the northernmost reaches of the state was the birthplace of Hale's Ales, founded in 1983 and brewed in Colville until 1991 (and presently thriving in the Ballard district of Seattle). These days, Colville is home to Lost Falls Brewing Co., and like Hale's was back in the early days of microbrewing, Lost Falls is located in a nondescript warehouse. In fact, you have to look pretty hard to find Lost Falls, but you will want to seek out this three-barrel brewery, as this is no typical brewery.

Public hours are limited to a few a day, Wednesdays through Fridays, but that doesn't stop the locals from arriving en masse to catch up with neighbors and sip from among owner Chip Trudell's delicious offerings. Within moments after officially opening at 4 p.m., the brewery turns into Party Central, with people bringing homemade casseroles, cookies, sausages, salads, and appetizers to share. Soon, folks are standing shoulder-to-shoulder, chatting and enjoying Lost Falls beers, which are poured on the far side of the brewery straight from the taps. The IPA, a solid version in the classic Northwest style, is the big seller. Trudell's rye beer is spicy with a crisp finish, and the rich porter is dessert in a glass. As more people show up, the place can get pretty loud and animated, but it's all in good fun and the enthusiasm is contagious. "It's a rock concert," one fan shouted over the din.

Trudell, who has been brewing since he was 14, has limited distribution for his Lost Falls beers, only because he can barely make enough to keep up with the thirsty locals who show up each week. Please contact Lost Falls before you stop by, and do make sure to be there when the place is open to the public. You will go for the beer, but stay for the fun.

DON'T MISS

- Ruud Awakening IPA or Hooligan Stout at Old Schoolhouse Brewery.
- The potluck party of locals when the doors open to the public each week at Lost Falls.

SOUTHEASTERN WASHINGTON

Snipes Mountain Brewing is named for Ben Snipes, a cattle rancher in the Yakima Valley in the mid-1800s. Snipes' modest cabin was located in a spot where he could keep an eye on his cattle empire and where travelers could stop for a meal and some rest before moving on. Snipes' namesakes brewpub is anything but modest, with lofty ceilings, large windows, and a glassed-in room where customers can watch the brewery in action. Snipes produces a wide variety of beers. The surprisingly flavorful Xtra

Blonde Ale is a favorite among the locals, and Coyote Moon is a well-constructed English brown ale. Head brewer Chris Miller enjoys dabbling; his seasonal beers are especially worth seeking, and he always has at

SNIPES MOUNTAIN BREWING CO.
905 Yakima Valley Hwy.
Sunnyside, 509-837-2739
snipesmountain.com

Snipes Mountain brews award-winning beers at its Sunnyside brewpub.

Beers from around the globe and around the neighborhood share space at West Richland Beer & Wine.

least one on tap. Miller keeps a few barrels onsite for barrel-aging beers, and he's also quite adept at working with Belgian yeast and additions of fresh fruits.

With an expansive selection of craft beer from around the world, across the country, and around the region, West Richland Beer & Wine is a nice stop in West Richland, a community that some locals refer to as the "fourth Tri-City." This bottle shop has six rotating taps, so you can enjoy a beer as you shop. It's a bit tough to find the small store, which is tucked away in a strip mall, but definitely worth the hunt.

ICE HARBOR BREWERY & PUB
206 N. Benton St.
Kennewick, 509-582-5340
iceharbor.com

In Kennewick, Ice Harbor Brewing Co.'s two locations mean locals never get thirsty for good beer. The original brewpub, established in 1997, has more local flavor; it's located in an old building alongside the railroad tracks. The two-story structure offers a lively bar and tables downstairs and a pool table up top. Order your beer by looking at the large chalkboard on the far end of the downstairs room that shows which beers from Ice Harbor's extensive lineup are available at the time; there are usually at least seven standard beers and a handful more seasonal and specialty brews to choose from, along with a cask selection. This brewpub has a mug club, and at any given time, at least four-fifths of the people in the place are drinking their beer from the special mugs reserved exclusively for members. Ice Harbor's newer spot, on the waterfront, offers more of a restaurant atmosphere.

"Laht Neppur" is "Ruppenthal" spelled backwards. That's the surname of the family that started Laht Neppur Brewing Co., a small brewery with "pub grub" on the side, in the equally small

town of Waitsburg. A homebrewer for years, Court Ruppenthal had moved with his wife, Katie, to the vineyards of Walla Walla Valley to learn winemaking; but the beer bug stuck with him as he worked with local winemakers. Realizing that the valley's winemakers needed a good brewer, Ruppenthal changed his focus and opened Laht Neppur in 2006. It's not just winemakers that meet in the eclectic space, though. The family-friendly brewpub is a welcome spot for locals as well as people who travel to the region for the vast outdoor recreation opportunities.

Miniature mugs hold the samples on Laht Neppur's ample taster tray.

LAHT NEPPUR BREWING CO.
444 Preston Ave.
Waitsburg, 509-337-6261
lahtneppur.com

Laht Neppur's dozen taps offer a selection of standard beers, such as the smooth yet roasty Oatmeal Porter, the sweet yet crisp Katie's Kölsch, and the malty Piper Canyon Scottish Ale, plus a handful of seasonal brews, which are available only for a short time.The aged Bonnie's Barley Wine is a complex brew with enough alcohol strength that customers are allowed only two per day. The refreshing Strawberry Cream Ale, with just a hint of fruit, was so popular in summer, it has been on tap ever since.

I found Whetstone Public House in Waitsburg while trying to locate Laht Neppur. The exterior looked inviting, so I thought I'd check it out (all in the name of research, of course). The interior was just as welcoming—sort of a cross between an old saloon and a Seattle alehouse. It was Peanut Night, so shells were scattered on the floor around all the occupied chairs as customers dove into the free peanuts. The clientele was very friendly, as was the helpful server, who even called Laht Neppur to make sure they would remain open for me. Whetstone has a small selection of taps, with a couple of craft beers from the area and a few more from the larger craft breweries like New Belgium. Old-fashioned coolers with large windows make a nice backdrop behind the bar and keep the selection of bottled beers cold. It's worth a stop if you are in the area enjoying the great outdoors—or en route to Laht Neppur.

DON'T MISS

• The seasonal beers at Snipes Mountain.

• The award-winning, best-selling Columbia Kölsch at Ice Harbor.

• Piper Canyon Scottish Ale or Katie's Kölsch at Laht Neppur.

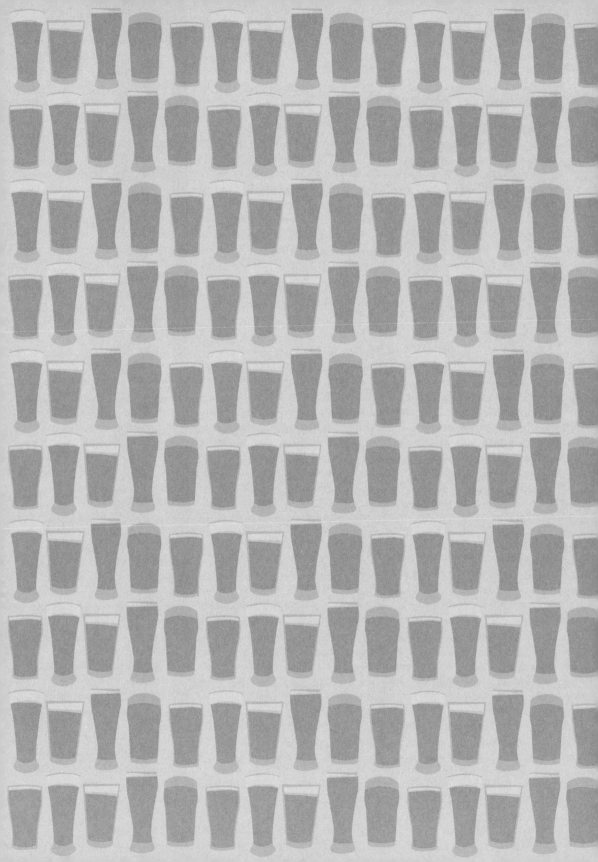

BRITISH COLUMBIA

BRITISH COLUMBIA

While not as high profile as Washington or Oregon artisan breweries, British Columbia brewers have taken part in the craft beer revolution: craft beers have been flourishing in British Columbia just as long as they have in the southern reaches of the Pacific Northwest, and thanks to some visionary beer pioneers, craft beer's roots are just as deep here.

One important item: note the name, British Columbia. The British influence is still felt in B.C., especially in the very provincial town of Victoria. And that includes a decidedly British accent in most of the craft beers. That's great news for fans of traditional malty British and German styles. There are more and more examples of extreme beers and brewers in B.C., but the beer culture here has a lighter palate than those in Oregon and Washington. Hopheads are hard-pressed in many parts of the province to find those bracingly bitter-in-a-good-way beers that are so prevalent and popular stateside. The sour beers such as Belgian- and French-style farmhouse ales that have been growing in popularity in Washington and Oregon aren't quite as prevalent in British Columbia, either. No doubt in part to the large number of Englanders who now call B.C, home, British beer styles, with their relatively more subtle flavors, reign supreme, with traditional German styles also making a jolly good showing. For those who love their hops, it can be a bit challenging, but for malt fans, it's a mecca. My suggestion to travelers accustomed to American hoppy beers is to enter B.C. with an open mind and a sense of adventure, and drink in all the region has to offer.

BEST FESTS: BRITISH COLUMBIA

Canada Cup of Beer
Vancouver
canadacupofbeer.com

Great Canadian Beer Festival
Victoria
gcbf.com

Hopscotch Scotch, Whisky & Beer Festival
Vancouver
hopscotchfestival.com

Kelowna Beer Festival
Kelowna
kelownabeerfest.com

Okanagan Fest of Ales
Penticton
fest-of-ale.bc.ca

VANCOUVER

An easy and interesting walk in downtown Vancouver will get you to six completely different beer establishments. They are so close to each other that you might not even be able to work up a thirst, so plenty of backtracking is always a possibility. Start anywhere, and know you won't starve: along the way are Chambar, an excellent Belgian restaurant, one of Vancouver's "top tastes," with a good tap and bottle selection, and the Irish Heather, a gastropub. Warning: you'll have to look closely to find the Railway Club, with its large tap selection and an emphasis on local craft brewers: it's on the second floor, above a convenience store.

THE CREAM ALE CONUNDRUM

Order a cream ale in the United States, and you will typically get a pint of light-colored beer that is also light in body and well carbonated and sometimes uses a mix of ale and lager yeast to induce a creamy texture in the mouth. Order a cream ale in Vancouver, and chances are good that the beer will more closely resemble an English brown ale, a reddish brown to dark brown brew that is malty, with some fruity or nutty characteristics and even some hints of chocolate.

Raven Cream Ale is often a dark, roasty surprise.

R & B Brewing Co.'s Raven Cream Ale is the culprit. A World Beer Cup award-winner, Raven is a popular beer that's on tap all over Vancouver and is changing the way Vancouverites think about cream ales. Light-colored and light-bodied cream ales? Quoth the Raven, "Nevermore!"

R & B Brewing Co.
54 E. Fourth Ave., Vancouver, 604-874-2537, r-and-b.com

PUB CRAWL: DOWNTOWN VANCOUVER

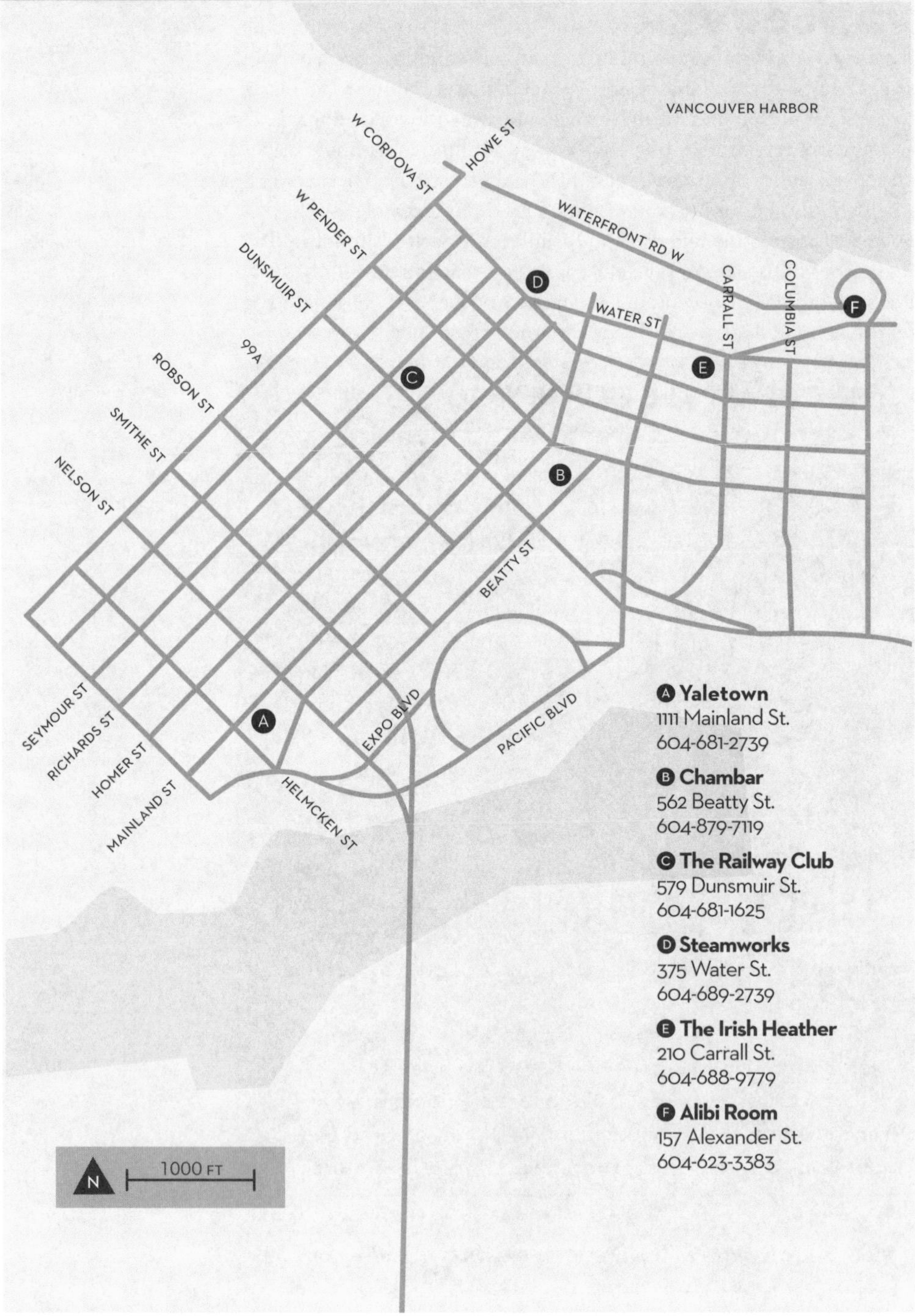
VANCOUVER HARBOR
W CORDOVA ST
HOWE ST
W PENDER ST
WATERFRONT RD W
DUNSMUIR ST
99A
ROBSON ST
SMITHE ST
NELSON ST
WATER ST
CARRALL ST
COLUMBIA ST
BEATTY ST
EXPO BLVD
PACIFIC BLVD
SEYMOUR ST
RICHARDS ST
HOMER ST
MAINLAND ST
HELMCKEN ST
A
B
C
D
E
F
N
1000 FT
A Yaletown
1111 Mainland St.
604-681-2739
B Chambar
562 Beatty St.
604-879-7119
C The Railway Club
579 Dunsmuir St.
604-681-1625
D Steamworks
375 Water St.
604-689-2739
E The Irish Heather
210 Carrall St.
604-688-9779
F Alibi Room
157 Alexander St.
604-623-3383

Let's start this Vancouver beer expedition where the city got its start, the Gastown District. Amid the cobblestone streets, bustling activity, and historic buildings, and just steps away from the world's first steam-powered clock, Steamworks Brewing Co. caters to locals, tourists, and curious cruise ship voyagers alike in the spacious multi-leveled brewpub and restaurant. Bypass the upper, street level and head downstairs, where English expatriates sip the British-style Empress IPA, and other denizens of this dark pub order the lager, pale ale, or "Berry White," a blend of Steamworks' Raspberry Frambozen and Ipanema, a wit that's brewed for the summer months. Hopheads will want to inquire if the North by Northwest Pale Ale is available; the servers apparently tend to "forget" when it's on tap. "It's the beer the staff wants to keep for themselves" says head brewer Conrad Gmoser. "They often will not mention it's on so they can have it after their shift."

The brewers tend to the small system right inside the pub, which is fired up by the same Gastown steam line that runs throughout the building and powers the famous clock. Brewing at Steamworks is a reality show waiting to happen; it takes place just several feet away without any walls or glass to come between brewer and imbiber. It can, at times, make for a boisterous bar setting, but it gives a wandering beer explorer something to

**STEAMWORKS
BREWING CO.**
375 Water St., Vancouver
604-689-2739,
steamworks.com

watch and talk about with the neighbors—plus, you have visual proof the beer is as local as it gets.

In true British form, Vancouverites call the Alibi Room a "free house," meaning it doesn't have any business ties to a brewpub or beer brand. Most pubs in Britain are "tied houses," at least partially owned by breweries, and are therefore—naturally—required to pour mostly if not exclusively that brewery's products. The free

The world's oldest steam clock marks the time—and the way to Steamworks. Photo © iStockphoto.com/Sergey Ivanov.

The Alibi Room raises the bar for good beer in Vancouver.

STORM BREWING CO.
310 Commercial Dr.
Vancouver, 604-255-9119
stormbrewing.org

house autonomy grants owners Raya Audet and Nigel Spring-thorpe the agility to rotate an amazing variety of beers on their 25 taps plus one rotating cask beer. Most hail from the province's growing number of breweries (many of the beers are exclusive to the Alibi Room), but they also reach beyond to other Canadian provinces, with an occasional American one-off keg miracu-lously making its way onto a waiting tap. This is the place to sample from B.C.'s best and brightest breweries, one of which is located pretty darn close, in gritty East Vancouver: if they're on, try any one of Storm Brewing's three fruit lambics—raspberry, blackberry, and black cherry. Some others to search for: Phillips, Tree, Crannóg, and Central City.

The Yaletown District, a former rough-and-tumble slice of the city, is the present home of urban trendsetters, dotted with chic boutiques, swanky bars and restaurants, and former warehouses now converted into SoHo-style lofts and live-work spaces. And here is also where you will find Yaletown Brewing Co. Established in 1994, Yaletown and the eponymous district where it resides grew up together, and the transition from exterior to interior is seamless, with gleaming stainless steel and dark wood creating a classy yet industrial setting. Head brewer Iain Hill has been with Yaletown, Vancouver's original brewpub, since inception. He is not just Yaletown's brewer; he is the head brewer for all the Mark James Group brewpubs that are scattered across the region.

YALETOWN BREWING CO.
1111 Mainland St.
Vancouver, 604-681-2739
markjamesgroup.com

Yaletown has a split personality. One half features a spacious restaurant for more intimate occasions; a lively pub takes up the other half, with sports on flat-screened TVs, a toasty fireplace, pool tables, and a lengthy gleaming bar, where patrons belly up for Hill's lineup of beers. Standout standards include Nagila Pale Ale, a British-influenced pale ale with Northwest hop notes, and Warehouse Stout, a smooth operator with hints of roasted coffee, chocolate, and a touch of smoke. Can't decide between the two? Hill offers Helmcken Black & Tan, the perfect balance of rich stout flavors blended with a touch of citrusy crispness. What really sets Yaletown apart, though, is Hill's love for and expertise in creating sour beers. If you are lucky, Hill will have his Oud Bruin Flemish

"DREAM BIG. WORK HARD. HAVE A BEER."

That's the motto of the Mark James Group, British Columbia's largest collection of craft brewpubs and restaurants.
Established in 1976, MJG has several brewery restaurants,
a handful of lounges, and even a clothing store, all in the
Greater Vancouver metropolitan area. Despite what could
easily have become a chain of cookie-cutter establishments,
the Mark James Group has done an admirable job of assur-
ing that each brewpub (Yaletown in Vancouver, Big Ridge
in Surrey, Flying Beaver in Richmond, Taylor's Crossing in
North Vancouver, and Whistler Brewhouse in Whistler) is
unique and a reflection of its neighborhood. Even the beers
are different in each establishment, save the ubiquitous
Red Truck Ale, which, although made at each brewery with
the same recipe, still varies slightly from place to place and
brewer to brewer. Visit them all at markjamesgroup.com.

*Yaletown's patio is a
popular destination.*

Sour Brown or some other sour delicacy on draft. On a pretty day,
take your beers out to the large patio and enjoy the Yaletown see-
and-be-seen scene.

DON'T MISS

- North by Northwest Pale Ale or the "Berry White" at Steamworks.
- Your choice from great breweries such as Storm, Tree, Phillips,
  Driftwood, and others at the Alibi Room.
- The varied Belgian-style beers at Yaletown.

SEA-TO-SKY HIGHWAY CORRIDOR

The original name for Whistler Mountain was London Mountain, named at least partially for the foggy, London-like weather that often shrouds the area. Some marketing geniuses decided that if a ski resort were going to take off, though, it shouldn't be associated with London's drizzly climate, and the moniker Whistler was chosen for the musical marmots that reside in the region, nicknamed "whistlers" for the calls they make.

Whistler is a playground, not only for sports enthusiasts but for gourmands, fashionistas, and folks who love the nightlife. From shopping and après-ski activities to zip lines, gondola rides, and world-class mountain biking, the pedestrian-friendly village offers enough of everything to work up a good thirst. Lucky then, that Whistler Brewhouse, the northernmost outpost of the Mark James Group of brewpubs, is conveniently located on one end of "the Village Stroll," the main walkway in the center of town. That's where brewer Dave Woodward creates magic in a minuscule brewpub that shares space with the pub and restaurant staff's winter sports equipment, at the ready for a quick schuss when shifts end.

Woodward's workspace might be small, but his passion is mighty. He cranks out an incredible amount of beer and varieties for a seemingly endless rush of thirsty patrons. No easy feat, considering his equipment, which is crammed into a space above the restaurant/pub area so tightly that Woodward must keep an eye on his waistline, else he might not be able to squeeze past the fermenters. It's an ironic situation, considering that the lodge-style establishment is quite spacious. During peak season, though, it is best to make reservations if you are planning on eating, because it can fill up quickly.

WHISTLER BREWHOUSE
4355 Blackcomb Way
Whistler, 604-905-2739
markjamesgroup.com

Whistler's brewmaster Dave Woodward squeezes out tasty beer in a tiny brewery.

Lifty Lager, light in flavor and color, is the house favorite, but Woodward and many regulars prefer the Big Wolf Bitter, especially on cask, with its complex British malt profile and zesty hop finish. Hopheads seek the 3D Double IPA, which Woodward says stands for "Damned Deceptively Drinkable." Unfortunately, it's a seasonal that shows up only on occasion. The Bear Arse Barley

Wine, another seasonal that appears only in the winter months, is a favorite among staff and beer hunters, perfect sipping by the fire in the pub side of the establishment. No matter what your pleasure, keep an eye on the prominently displayed light board that reveals the status of each beer. A green light signifies there is plenty of that brew, yellow stands for a beer that's getting low, and a red light means you better order up before it's gone.

Insider tip: it's easy to confuse Whistler Brewhouse with Whistler Brewing Co., a production brewery that built a small brewery in Whistler before the 2010 Olympics after operating in Vancouver for years. You want the MJG brewpub that is right on "the stroll."

A visit to Howe Sound Brewing in the quaint town of Squamish is a must either going to or coming from Whistler, serendipitously situated between it and the big city of Vancouver. In fact, after a visit to the Whistler Brewhouse and then a tour of that resort village, you might choose to make the drive to Squamish and spend the night at Howe Sound; not only is it an award-winning brewpub, it's also an inn with 20 guest rooms. The wood building was erected specifically for Howe Sound Brewing, which opened its doors in 1996. John Mitchell, the "Grandfather of Canadian Craft Brewing," was the first brewer for the family-run operation. In addition to the brewery and guest rooms, the building offers a pub, restaurant, and banquet and business facilities, many with breathtaking views of the majestic mountains that grace the region.

HOWE SOUND BREWING
37801 Cleveland Ave.
Squamish, 800-919-2537
howesound.com

With both the mountains and Howe Sound (North America's southernmost fjord) so close by, this particular brewery is surrounded by a plethora of outdoor recreational activities, no matter what the season. You might just want to enjoy some physical activity to help burn off calories—a goodly number of delicious brews are made at Howe Sound. If you can't try them all onsite, never fear: many of Howe Sound's beers are available in regional beer stores in distinctive one-liter bottles that come capped and sporting a swing-top, so the beer can be resealed to finish later. Try the beers on draft at the bright and airy lodge-styled pub and plan to take some bottles along for later sipping. The Garibaldi Honey Pale Ale is an award-winner that would please a malt lover looking for a lighter-flavored quaff. Hopheads will want to seek the Baldwin & Cooper Best Bitter (named for the men that first climbed the nearby Grand Wall of the Stawamus Chief) and Devil's Elbow IPA, by far the hoppiest of the lot, weighing in at a respectable 68 IBUs. If you are really lucky, the gently spiced and deftly balanced Father John's Winter Ale (named for Mitchell) will be on tap. With subtle hints of seasonal spices, it's like a holiday cookie in a glass. If it's not on tap, the kitchen might be making ice

(Left) Howe Sound offers beers on draft and in specially designed swing-top and capped bottles. (Right) Howe Sound's Father John's Winter Ale is a tribute to beer pioneer John Mitchell.

cream with it; many of Howe Sound's beers are transformed into tasty frozen treats.

On any run along the Sea-to-Sky Corridor, you can check out several other establishments. Taylor's Crossing, part of the Mark James Group, is the North Shore's only brewpub; it features about six of its own craft brews on tap along with a seasonal special or two. The Avalon Cold Beer & Wine Store is attached to Taylor's Crossing, so you can explore some other local and regional craft beers in bottles as well. Sailor Hagar's Brew Pub really isn't a brewpub; it features 18 draft beers from around the world, six of which are beers handcrafted from the pub's original recipes, but the beers are no longer brewed onsite, instead being contract-brewed by Howe Sound. Try the Lohin's ESB, an extra special bitter in the English tradition with a nice extra hint of hops. It's named for Sailor Hagar's original brewer, Gary Lohin, a well-known and respected brewer who is now working his magic at Central City Brewing in the Vancouver suburb of Surrey. Sailor Hagar's also has a cold beer and wine store just down the street, if you'd rather take a beer or two to go for later enjoyment.

TAYLOR'S CROSSING

1035 Marine Dr., North Vancouver, 604-986-7899
markjamesgroup.com

CENTRAL CITY BREWING

13450 102nd Ave.
Surrey, 604-582-6620
centralcitybrewing.com

DON'T MISS

- 3D Double IPA, Bear Arse Barley Wine, and the beer-status light board at Whistler Brewhouse.
- Father John's Winter Ale, Devil's Elbow IPA, and beer ice cream at Howe Sound.

VANCOUVER ISLAND

VICTORIA

You can't really get much more British in North America than Victoria. For a city of its size, this picturesque provincial port town

BEER PIONEERS:
JOHN MITCHELL AND FRANK APPLETON

Two transplanted Brits, John Mitchell and Frank Appleton, are considered the chief pioneers in Canada's craft beer culture. John Mitchell got the idea to start a small, independent brewery while visiting his homeland in the early 1980s. While there, he learned that only a small handful of pub-breweries still existed in Britain, where just a century before, there had been more than 12,000 dotting the country. Those small, independent breweries and their ardent fans were committed to reviving the tradition of brewing craft beer, and, recognizing that a similar situation was happening in Canada, Mitchell returned to British Columbia with a commitment to create similar change there.

Mitchell met up with Appleton, a former brewer who had been working as a consultant in B.C., and they set about building the first brewpub in Canada. Mitchell handled the government dealings, convincing bureaucrats and politicians that granting permission for this newfangled idea would be beneficial, while Appleton worked on the brewery and test brews. Within several months, everything fell into place, and Horseshoe Bay Brewing opened for business in summer of 1982. Mitchell and Appleton both left Horseshoe shortly afterward (it has since closed), but they continued to work together on spawning other breweries throughout B.C. and are credited for inspiring the launch of numerous brewpubs and craft breweries throughout Canada.

is home to an impressive number of British-style pubs and craft breweries and brewpubs. The downtown literally buzzes throughout all hours of the day and well into the night with tourists and residents, but it's a relaxed pace, with the very British tradition of afternoon tea (or a pint at a favorite local pub) considered to be a necessary part of the day for many.

One such British gentleman, Ken Franklin, kept me company at the Canoe Brewpub, Marina, and Restaurant one sunny afternoon, among the brightly colored sails in the marina, as I sipped one of Canoe's River Rock Bitters, a British-style extra special bitter that is a true session beer. Franklin said that his "local" used to be another pub in town, but one day, the servers told him they could no longer pour his pint up to the rim, as was his preference, because the bottom-line-oriented new management stipulated a lesser pour. He talked to the new manager, who confirmed that the establishment would only serve pints with head room. Franklin stormed out, wandered down the street to Canoe, ordered his beer the way he likes it, and continues to get his perfectly poured pint every day.

Attention to customer service is evident at Canoe, as is attention to the beer, whether it is one of the four standard beers such as Beaver Brown Ale, a sturdy yet drinkable English brown ale, or Siren Song Pale Ale, with hints of Northwest hops; one of the rotating seasonals, such as Habit, an espresso stout brewed with beans from a local coffee purveyor; or the 2008 Canadian Brewing Awards gold medalist, Bavarian Copper Bock, a bready German bock.

Canoe is housed in the City Lights Building, erected in 1894 to power Victoria's streetlights. Coal-fired electric generators created the spark that kept the city's inner harbor powered up for decades and stood as a proud landmark on the downtown waterfront. When the founders of Canoe got to it, though, in 1996, the building had sat empty for years, enduring the slow decay that many historic buildings see over decades of neglect. The owners put the building through a massive restoration, retrofit, and rejuvenation. Two years and six million dollars later, Canoe opened, nicely juxtaposing the building's soaring timber frame and rustic brick architecture with sparkling crystal chandeliers—truly a stunning setting for a meal, a beer, and great conversation with friends, old

Canoe customers drink in the view and the wide range of beers, from smooth Red Canoe Lager to rich Habit espresso stout.

and new. Being both a restaurant and a brewpub meant the existing space had to be used judiciously, so head brewer Sean Hoyne, who was brought into the project to build the brewery, stuck the serving tanks on a loft above the pub, a constant visual reminder that the beer is as local as it gets.

As you stroll along Victoria's center, you will no doubt stumble across a small park—a tiny triangular patch of land, actually—situated in the strangely shaped intersection of Wharf and Johnson streets. There's a park bench there, and it always has at least one occupant. It's a sculpture, life-sized and full-bodied, of Michael Williams, the visionary who founded Swans Suite Hotel and Brew Pub from a rundown old warehouse that once was the feed store where Williams got food for the border collies he bred and raised. In addition to Swans, Williams is credited with redeveloping most of the surrounding area in an effort to preserve the historic buildings.

Swans brewer Andrew Tessier created a special beer as a tribute to Williams, who died in 2000, and again for Swans' 20th anniversary in 2009. At 10 percent ABV, it's a barley wine that demands slow sipping and enjoyment. Aged with Spanish orange peel and pieces of oak ("chunks, actually," according to Tessier) that are thrown into the fermenter and left there, each batch of the Williams tribute beer, appropriately named Legacy Ale, changes slightly with time as the wood continues to impart its flavor. Legacy is rarely available on draft, but Tessier makes sure bottles are available in the adjacent beer and wine store. He also usually stashes some away with other bottles in the brewpub's cooler for patrons who are in the know. But you have to find the right bartender; it's such a well-kept secret that even some of the pub staff doesn't know about the bottles. Take a glass of Legacy with you and sip on it slowly, letting it warm up as you go on a self-guided walking tour throughout Swans and its First Nations art and artifacts, including a dramatic, towering totem pole, that were all part of Williams' private collection.

Tessier's other beers include Arctic Ale, a light-flavored blonde that is the most popular pour in the brewpub, followed by the tasty, toasty Coconut Porter and a seasonal Pumpkin Ale. The

A statue of Swans founder Michael Williams sits and watches over his creation.

SWANS BUCKERFIELD BREWERY
506 Pandora Ave.
Victoria, 250-361-3310
swanshotel.com/pub.php

A MATTER OF MEASUREMENTS

Ordering a beer in British Columbia can be a confusing adventure. In Victoria, especially, the British influence means that beer is available in three sizes at many places: a pint is typically of the 20-ounce Imperial variety; a sleeve is 16 ounces (what Americans think of as a pint); and a glass is a half-pint, or 10 ounces. In other parts of B.C., beer can be seen served in liters and half-liters, or pints that are either 16 ounces or 20 ounces, and also in half-pints or glasses. One rule of thumb is that the further inland you travel, the more apt pubs are to lose the British measurements. Pitchers tend to be more prevalent in B.C.'s interior, along with draft towers—tall, beaker-looking devices designed for larger groups. A draft tower holds seven pints and comes complete with its own chiller to keep the beer cold and a spigot on the bottom for tabletop dispensing.

SPINNAKERS
308 Catherine St.
Victoria, 877-838-2739
spinnakers.com

Riley's Scotch Ale, sweet, smooth, and deceptively 8 percent ABV, is among the fuller-bodied beers in all of British Columbia.

It's a pleasant mile-long walk across the Johnson Street Bridge ("Big Blue" to locals) to Spinnakers. Spinnakers is more than Canada's oldest brewpub. The considerable complex features lush gardens; an in-house specialty food merchant that sells house-made cheeses, vinegars, breads, and chocolates; a malt vinegar brewery; and an artisan bakery, which also supplies baked goods for the restaurant and even turns out handmade dog treats. The folks at Spinnakers also bottle their own proprietary water straight

Swans brewer Andrew Tessier with Legacy, a barley-wine tribute to the man who built the brewery.

from an on-premises aquifer. And Spinnakers offers several guest houses, either in its restored 1884 historic-registered Victorian-era house or in an adjacent multiplex with suites that can include kitchens, fireplaces, and Jacuzzis. Kind of a McMenamins of the North!

The brewers make about 25 different ales, lagers, and seasonal beers each year and have been known to dive deep into the brew books to "find out what we forgot," says publican (and the original architect for the brewpub) Paul Hadfield, adding that, at any given time, the brewers might decide to whip up a Spinnakers original beer, such as Abbot Ale, which was created by John Mitchell and first brewed in 1984. "We have, perhaps, seven or eight beers all the time, and we mess around on the other three taps the rest of the time and bring some fun, some seasonality, to the whole notion of drinking beer."

Spinnakers is a must-visit destination for any beer lover.

Whether they are a new creation, a long-lost recipe, or a perennial favorite, many Spinnakers ales are served by hand-pumped beer engines imported from England. These traditional ales are served at what is often called "cellar temperature," about 53 degrees, which helps to bring out the beers' flavors and aromas. The traditional touch is especially welcomed with the chocolaty Mt. Tolmie Dark, an updated version of Mitchell's 20th brew at Spinnakers in 1984; the traditional British-style beers like Mitchell's Extra Special Bitter, a favorite among the regulars; and the darker and richer seasonals.

Spinnakers European- and American-style lagers and some ales—such as the Kölsch-style ale, the lightest offering, another old-timer known as Spinnakers Ale, and newcomer Blue Bridge Double IPA—are served with more carbonation at a colder 38 degrees. In addition, a small cask, called a firkin, of beer is tapped each weeknight at Spinnakers, something different every day. Before the days of artificial carbonation, beer went through a secondary fermentation in these small wooden casks, and the beer was then served fresh from the firkin. Cask night is a big draw across Victoria and Vancouver, with weekly cask nights on tap at many locations. But Spinnakers is the only establishment that taps a fresh cask five days a week.

If you don't book a room, at least plan to stay for a meal at Spinnakers. Hadfield has been a leader in sustainable practices at Spinnakers since the early 1990s, with a focus on local sourcing for ingredients in the restaurant. The menu changes seasonally to accommodate what is available from the growing number of

Local Kitchen pours local beers such as those from the innovative Driftwood Brewery.

Phillips Brewing is an island favorite.

DRIFTWOOD BREWERY
450 Hillside Ave.
Victoria, 250-381-2739
driftwoodbeer.com

PHILLIPS BREWING CO.
2010 Government St.
Victoria, 877-380-1912
phillipsbeer.com

LIGHTHOUSE BREWING CO.
2-836 Devonshire Rd.
Victoria, 250-383-6500
lighthousebrewing.com

VANCOUVER ISLAND BREWERY,
2330 Government St.
Victoria, 250-361-0007
vanislandbrewery.com

local and regional farms that Spinnakers works with to source only the freshest ingredients. You will not see a fresh tomato on the menu in winter, for instance, because they are not available on the island. Instead, the menu at Spinnakers will feature recipes with the tomatoes that were canned when they were abundant in summer. It has been a long road for Hadfield to get to a point where nearly all the food he serves in his restaurant comes from a short way away, but it is part of what he believes Spinnakers stands for. "We are artisans in brewing, and in food as well," he says.

It's a scenic trek from Spinnakers back into the downtown area, where you'll appreciate Local Kitchen, a restaurant with a smaller but well-planned selection of taps catering to the city's local breweries: Driftwood, Phillips, Lighthouse, and Vancouver Island. While there are other pubs to enjoy in the area, you must make a point of visiting one of Canada's oldest: tucked in Bastion Square, Garrick's Head has been serving beer to locals and tourists since 1867 and is known today for a wide selection of local and regional craft beer.

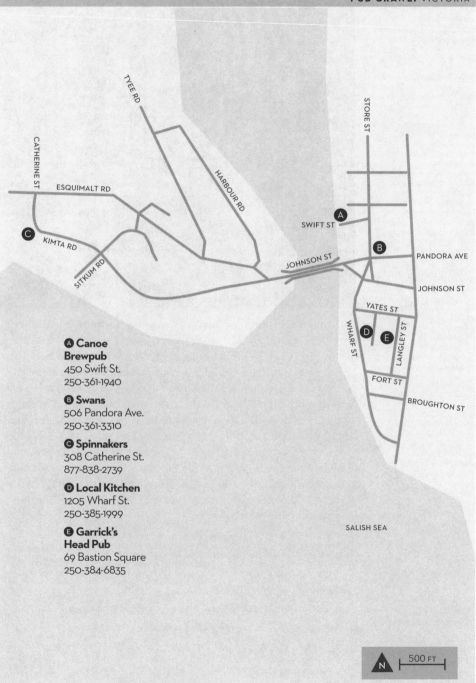

A Canoe Brewpub
450 Swift St.
250-361-1940

B Swans
506 Pandora Ave.
250-361-3310

C Spinnakers
308 Catherine St.
877-838-2739

D Local Kitchen
1205 Wharf St.
250-385-1999

E Garrick's Head Pub
69 Bastion Square
250-384-6835

Six Mile Pub has been quenching the thirsts of beer fans for more than 150 years.

If you feel like getting behind the wheel in this easy-walking town, two neighborhood pubs are worth a visit for their historic value as well as the beer. Consistently listed among the best pubs in Victoria, Christie's Carriage House has been serving thirsty locals and travelers since 1986 in a large Queen Anne–style house that was built in 1898 by local carriage maker Eldridge Christie; with 25 beers on tap, there's sure to be something to please just about everybody. And Six Mile Pub, established in 1855 (six miles from downtown Victoria), is the oldest pub in British Columbia. Popular with bootleggers during Prohibition, Six Mile now caters to locals and visitors who flock to the eclectic pub to drink in the 22 draft beers on tap, watch hockey on the big-screen TVs, and enjoy authentic British fare.

DON'T MISS

- Sipping a beer on Canoe's splendid outdoor patio or directly beneath the serving vessels.
- Toasting Michael Williams with a Legacy Ale at Swans.
- Weeknight cask-tapping at Spinnakers.
- Locally made beers at the Local Kitchen.
- Soaking up some history at Christie's Carriage House and Six Mile Pub.

THE REST OF THE ISLAND

It's a bit of a beer desert past Victoria, but there are two places on the island that are worth a visit, if you are heading to points north.

Situated less than an hour's drive from Victoria, many commuters choose to live in the quiet and quaint city of Duncan. With a downtown that features a number of heritage and vintage buildings, and an interesting selection of shops and restaurants, it's easy to see why. Duncan is also home to a collection of 80 First Nations totem poles. You can take a self-guided tour and wind up at Craig Street Brew Pub, the only craft brewery between Victoria and Nanaimo, opened in 2006. Craig Street makes its home in a recently renovated 1940s building, with a warm interior that includes large, exposed timbers and a century-old Irish bar that Liz and Lance Steward, who also own the adjacent restaurant, bought at auction.

The space is deceiving. At first glance, it seems small, even when the outdoor streetside patio is in use. But travel up the spectacular staircase to find the brewhouse encased in two stories of glass. The mezzanine, with its historical photos of the region, offers a place to enjoy a brew or two in a quiet environment. The top floor is home to what staffers call "the library." Specially designed for larger groups, it is a semi-private room with big-screen TVs that can do double duty, displaying power-point presentations or the big game. There's even a rooftop patio. Craig Street brewer Chris Gress makes four year-round beers along with a handful of seasonals. I was charmed by the Craig Street Toolbox, a six-compartment wooden box that holds tasters of all four regular brews plus the current seasonal selection and a taster glass of

CRAIG STREET BREW PUB
45 Craig St.
Duncan, 250-746-5622
craigstreet.ca

Craig Street's "toolbox" is a clever taster tray.

(Above) Barry Ladell doesn't rush Longwood's beer. Ales mature for 21 days; lagers for more than one month. (Below) Longwood's framboise is a favorite at the pub and in the bottle.

LONGWOOD BREWPUB

5775 Turner Rd.
Nanaimo, 250-729-8225
longwoodbrewpub.com

5.0 %
ALC/VOL.

650 mL

BREWER   *Handcrafted*   PUBLICAN

Brewed & Bottled by Longwood Brew Pub, Nanaimo BC

peanuts to snack on.

Another 30 miles (48 km) north on Highway 1 gets you to Nanaimo, one of the towns serviced by BC Ferries. It's a short drive from the ferry terminal to Longwood, central Vancouver Island's original brewpub. Publican Barry Ladell has a long history in craft brewing in British Columbia. After many years working and traveling extensively as a brewery consultant, Ladell took one last gig to design Longwood's efficient brewery. Construction began in 1999 and Longwood opened in 2000. Somewhere along the line, Ladell, who was from the area, decided to buy into the brewpub and took on the job of being Longwood's publican because he wanted to settle back down in his hometown.

Longwood, which is also a restaurant and pub, is located in an upscale shopping mall, but once inside, it's easy to forget that location, thanks to the rich, dark wood and elegant interior design. The beers are generally made in the British style, with the IPA being a bit hoppier (refreshingly so) than many of the others on the island. The No. 1 draft is the Czech Pilsner, with its blonde Longwood Ale and the IPA weighing in a close second and third. If the imperial stout is on draft, it's a must-try beer. The ESB is another of John Mitchell's original recipes and is still brewed to his specifications by Longwood's head brewer Harley Smith—proof once again that this beer pioneer's influences are still felt across the island and the mainland.

DON'T MISS

- Craig Street's toolbox taster tray.
- John Mitchell's sublime ESB or the imperial stout at Longwood.

SOUTHERN INTERIOR

PENTICTON

Getting to Penticton is a glorious ride, flanked by majestic mountains and cliffs that border a pair of pristine lakes, through the southern end of British Columbia's Okanagan Valley. Long famous for its orchards, as grape vines take over aging fruit trees, the valley is increasingly known for its wineries; along one stretch of Highway 97, also known as the Wine Route, you drive past 15 of the valley's 100 wineries in the span of ten minutes. It might be considered unusual, then, that Penticton is home to one of the province's oldest and most popular beer festivals, a brewpub, and two production breweries.

Patt Dyck, who owns the Cannery Brewing Co. with her husband, Ron, knows why craft beer continues to grow steadily in this wine-soaked region. It's the old saying, "It takes a lot of great beer to make good wine." The truth behind this truism, she says, is shown by the number of local winemakers and their employees who sip on Cannery's beers throughout the year, especially during the hot, arduous harvest and winemaking season. "Wine is the extra in life. Beer replaces what life takes out," Dyck says, as a steady stream of locals gathers inside the brewery's small tasting room for a beer sample or to pick up cases of beer to go. Try the Maple Stout, if the seasonal beer is available. The addition of natural maple rounds out roasted bitterness from the grains and adds a decidedly Canadian touch to this beer with British roots. Rich in caramel and toffee-nut flavors, Naramata Nut Brown is a year-round offering worth a try. Dyck says it is so popular, residents of the nearby community, Naramata, tell visitors that the Cannery is located there instead of Penticton.

CANNERY BREWING CO.
112-1475 Fairview Rd.
Penticton, 250-493-2723
cannerybrewing.com

The Cannery cans its beer, of course. But the brewery also bottles.

**TIN WHISTLE
BREWING CO.**
954 W. Eckhardt St.
Penticton, 250-770-1122

You can find beers from the Cannery and the other brewery in town, Tin Whistle, plus a host of other B.C. brews at the Kettle Valley Station Pub, located adjacent to the Ramada Inn. A wood-fire oven heats up one end while a fireplace does the duty on the other side of this roomy pub and restaurant. Big-screen TVs help you keep tabs on all the sports, and the place can get pretty raucous when the Vancouver Canucks are on the ice. The staff is very friendly and excited to talk about beer, even though the usual focus in the area is on wine. Ask for a sampler tray that features your choice of four of the B.C. beers that are on tap. With about 15 taps in all, some from the U.S. and other provinces as well, there will always be something worthy of a taste or two.

Kettle Valley Station Pub is named for the Kettle Valley Rail-road, a now-defunct railway that once connected the small towns in the Okanagan. A good portion of the railroad's route has been converted to the Kettle Valley Rail Trail, used daily by hikers, cyclists, and other recreationalists. Another portion of the railway has been restored and is now used by the Kettle Valley Steam Railway, based in Summerland, which runs a restored 1912 steam locomotive along ten miles of tracks for hundreds of families and school children each year.

Summerland is also the home of an upscale restaurant, Local Lounge and Grille, which comes highly recommended by locals. Just a few miles from Penticton, Local features only six beer taps, but they all hail from nearby breweries. You can enjoy a cold one on the large deck, which overlooks Okanagan Lake, inside the very modern restaurant or upstairs in the swanky lounge. But if you want a really cold one, make sure to order the ice cream that is made in-house with local beers. The version made from the Cannery's Maple Stout is worth the trip to Summerland on its own if the area's beauty doesn't call you first.

DON'T MISS

- Maple Stout and other great beers at the Cannery tasting room.
- Sampler tray of B.C. beers at Kettle Valley Station Pub.
- Beer ice cream at Local Lounge and Grill.

KELOWNA

Kelowna is the largest city in the tourist-friendly Okanagan Valley, and home to one of the biggest surprises discovered while researching this book. Tucked away across the lake in West Kelow-na, 13 Monks was encountered only because it was connected to the hotel where my friends and research companions, Dan and

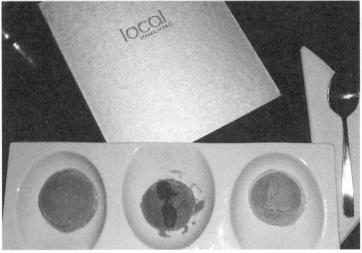

(Above) Wood-fired pizzas and beer samples at Kettle Valley Station Pub. (Below) A really cold one: "Locally" sourced beer in an ice cream treat.

Susan Bartlett, and I were staying. The establishment used to be a beer-oriented Fogg & Suds franchise, but owners Ryan English and Colleen Dubois decided not to renew the franchise agreement and set out on their own. They knew they wanted to keep the restaurant's focus on beer, but they changed the brightly colored interior to something more natural and low-key with lots of warm wood, rock facades, and gleaming metal. They also updated the beer menu. Within only a few months after opening, 13 Monks offers 15 beers and one cider on draft, plus 120 different bottled beers.

The emphasis at 13 Monks is on local beers, with selections from Kamloops Brewery, the Cannery, Tree Brewing, Tin Whistle, and more. A sampler tray allows you to choose six taster-size

KAMLOOPS BREWERY
965 McGill Place
Kamloops, 250-851-2543

13 Monks co-owner Ryan English is a beer educator as well as a restaurateur.

glasses from the taps, a great way for tourists and newer craft beer fans to explore the local breweries. There's also an impressive selection of imports among the bottled beer selection, with some rarer and interesting Belgian, Scottish, and British beers in the lineup. 13 Monks boasts that it is the only place in the Okanagan Valley that serves the white-labeled Chimay Tripel.

The owners have also incorporated beer into their menu items. One dessert features a large bowl, with a large martini glass in the center, surrounded by fresh raspberries. A large scoop of vanilla ice cream sits in the martini glass. The server pours a bottle of Morte Subite Framboise raspberry beer over the ice cream, allowing the pink, frothy liquid to cascade over the sides of the glass and onto the raspberries below. It's a beautiful and decadent dessert that helps introduce beer in a new way to 13 Monks' patrons. Not an easy task, according to English, who says it is a struggle trying to raise the respectability of beer in an area that is so closely linked to the wine industry. "It's getting better," he says. "The Kelowna and Penticton beer festivals have done a lot to raise awareness."

So has 13 Monks, and with plans to do more cooking and pairing food with beer on 13 Monks' menus, plus continued education among staff so they can help customers make good beer choices, the future looks promising.

TREE BREWING

1083 Richter St.
Kelowna, 250-717-1091
treebeer.com

One hophead haven in this part of B.C. is Tree Brewing, which has been brewing Hop Head IPA for more than a decade. With a citrusy grapefruit nose and flavors of more citrus balanced with some malty sweetness, Hop Head is credited by a lot of Canadian beer fans as being the first hoppy beer they loved. Consistently an award-winner, it has carved out enough of a niche for itself as a specialty brew to make it Tree's No. 1–selling bottled beer.

Hop Head has been so successful that Tree has branched out to two other Hop Head specialty brews. The original Hop Head was released in 2000, with 60 IBUs. In 2008, Tree released Hop Head Double IPA, one of the rare double IPAs in British Columbia. It's a big, rounded, nicely balanced hop bomb that's 8 percent ABV and around 85 IBUs. When its double IPA took gold in 2009 at the Canadian Brewing Awards, Tree decided to release another Hop Head on the heels of that success. Hop Head 45 is a red ale made with crystal and chocolate malt, so that it's a lot more malt forward but still has a clean hop finish. It clocks in with 45 IBUs and is oak-aged for 45 days.

Tree's other creations are equally delightful—it's just that finding a significantly hoppy beer in these parts warrants some fanfare. In Kelowna only, look for Beach Blonde Lager on draft in most pubs and restaurants. It's a very light, easy-drinking lager designed to entice the local macrobrew crew to explore craft beer. The Thirsty Beaver Amber is also very approachable, with a malty presence and a light hop finish. The Spy Porter incorporates all-chocolate malt to create a mellow, smooth flavor that doesn't have any roasted bitterness. And, Tree also brews a special lager especially for Gasthaus on the Lake, an authentic German restaurant in neighboring Peachland that is worth a visit if you're thirsting for some Bavarian beverages.

DON'T MISS

- The extensive beer list and Morte Subite Framboise dessert at 13 Monks.
- Tree Brewing's trio of Hop Heads.

SALMON ARM AND BEYOND

The moment you walk into Barley Station in Salmon Arm, you can tell that it is a locals place, but this brewpub also caters to the throngs of tourists who head to the region, especially in the summer months, to participate in all its recreational opportunities. The Tudor-style building is spacious, with plenty of windows that let in a good deal of light, keeping the dark wood of the pub from becoming too brooding.

Wit is a rare style in this region, and that's a shame, because the warm summer months and the wide variety of outdoor activities they inspire would pair perfectly with a crisp wit. Barley Station's version, Talking Dog Wit, is a good example of this Belgian style, with just enough coriander and orange peel to be refreshing and not cloying. Interestingly, Barley Station has another beer that is often thought of as an "easy drinker," its Station House

BARLEY STATION
20 Shuswap St. SE
Salmon Arm, 250-832-0999
barleystation.com

(Above) Brewmaster Stefan Buhl and managing director Tod Melnyk show off Tree Brewing's No. 1 bottled beer. (Below) Barley Station's colorful sampler tray catches the ample light.

Blonde; but at 5.1 percent ABV, it's the strongest in the brewery's regular lineup of beers, so take heed and remember: just because it's lighter in color doesn't mean it's lighter in alcohol.

Sam McGuire is a historic figure in Salmon Arm. So it's fitting that Barley Station named its standout beer, Sam McGuire's Pale Ale, for this local hero. A true Northwest-style pale ale, this award-winning beer is literally hopping with hop aroma as it reaches your lips, but it still keeps its balance with six different malts. Sam's is dry-hopped to give it the expected Northwest floral and citrusy overtones. It's an enjoyable brew, and at a mere 4.7 percent ABV, you can enjoy two—a splendid finale to any of the fun excursions the beautiful country surrounding Salmon Arm has to offer.

The highly lauded Crannóg Ales is about a half-hour drive from Salmon Arm. It is Canada's only Certified Organic farmhouse microbrewery, with exclusively B.C. distribution—only about as far away from the brewery as owners Brian MacIsaac and Rebecca Kneen can drive and still keep up with the farm and brewery. It is possible to visit Crannóg, but you must make an appointment to do so. Otherwise, take heart: you will definitely be able to enjoy Crannóg's beers at several locations throughout the province.

Another area brewery is Mt. Begbie, in Revelstoke, about an hour's drive from Salmon Arm. Like Crannóg, Mt. Begbie's beers, such as Selkirk Stout and High Country Kölsch, are available on draft and in bottles throughout the province.

CRANNÓG ALES
Sorrento, 250-675-6847
crannogales.com

MT. BEGBIE BREWING CO.
521 First St. W.
Revelstoke, 250-837-2756
mt-begbie.com

HOP HISTORY: ALEXANDER KEITH'S IPA

Despite its PacNW location, British Columbia has very few craft beer renditions of the region's favored beer style, India pale ale. And even fewer of those are hoppy enough to please a hophead's tough palate. If you are going through lupulin withdrawal in B.C., blame Alexander Keith's, a beer brand that was founded in Halifax, Nova Scotia, in 1820, making it one of the oldest beer brands in North America.

Alexander Keith's continues to brew its IPA to historic standards, not the ones that have evolved since craft brewers made the style so wildly popular. Any craft beer fan will point out that Alexander Keith's IPA only faintly resembles modern IPA standards. At 5 percent ABV, its strength is lower than the usual IPA, which usually comes in at around 6 to 7 percent ABV. Plus, Alexander Keith's has only 20 IBUs, compared to the 40 to 100 or more IBUs in craft IPAs. It also lacks the fruity and citrusy aromas that are common among modern IPAs.

Because Alexander Keith's is ubiquitous across British Columbia, though, most brewers believe they have to tone down their IPAs to better match the locals' perception of what an IPA really is.

DON'T MISS

- Barley Station's Sam McGuire Pale Ale.
- Crannóg Ales—but please make an appointment. Or try any of their draft-only organic ales, on tap around the province (Back Hand of God Stout is a real standout).
- Mt. Begbie Selkirk Stout and High Country Kölsch, available in many cold beer & wine stores.

A CASE FOR "COLD BEER & WINE" STORES

Finding bottled craft beers isn't difficult in British Columbia, but to the traveler, it can be a bit confusing. First off, there are the B.C. Government Liquor Stores, also called BCLS; in these, you can find a limited variety of craft beers among the large industrial and regional beers. But, according to Rick Green, B.C. beer blogger and president of Vancouver's CAMRA chapter, "I've never seen cold beer sold in a BCLS." There are a bunch of easily accessible BCLS locations, and now you pretty much know what not to expect when you get there. Don't expect cold beer!

Enter the privately licensed "cold beer & wine" stores. The amount and variety of craft beers available in these shops can range from drop-on-your-knees amazing to down-right boring, depending on the passions of the proprietor. Just like any other privately owned shops, the locations vary greatly—from strip malls to downtown storefronts—and the hours vary as well, although they do tend to stay open longer than the government stores. But, true to that lead adjective, you can at least take heart that the beer at any cold beer & wine store has been stored in a cool location.

Also note that many brewpubs have their own "stores" of cold beer and wine, so if you like a beer at a brewpub, check to see if you can pick some up to go, too.

PUB   BREWERY   BREWPUB   RESTAURANT   BREWERY/ TASTING ROOM

Please contact all breweries ahead of time if you plan to visit.

 **OREGON**

ASTORIA

Rogue Ales Public House
100 39th St. (Pier 39)
503-325-5964
www.rogue.com

BEND

Abbey Pub
1740 NW Pence Lane
541-323-2337

Blacksmith Restaurant
211 NW Greenwood Ave.
541-318-0588
www.bendblacksmith.com

Boneyard Beer
37 NW Lake
541-323-2325
boneyardbeer.com

Brother Jon's Public House
1227 NW Galveston Ave.
541-306-3321

The Lodge
1441 SW Chandler Ave.
541-388-4998
www.cascadelakes.com

Old St. Francis School
700 NW Bond St.
877-661-4228
www.mcmenamins.com

10 Barrel Brewing
1135 NW Galveston
541-678-5228
www.10barrel.com

CANNON BEACH

Warren House
3301 S. Hemlock St.
503-436-1130

CARLTON

Fire Mountain Brew House
10800 Rex Brown Rd.
503-852-7378

CENTRAL POINT

Walkabout Brewing
5204 Dobrot Way
541-858-5723

CORVALLIS

Impulse Bar & Grill
1425 NW Monroe Ave.
541-230-1114

Squirrel's Tavern
100 SW Second St.
541-753-8057
www.squirrelstavern.com

Suds & Suds
1045 NW Kings Blvd.
541-752-5151
www.woodstocks.com

ESTACADA

Fearless Brewing
326 S. Broadway
503-630-2337
www.fearless1.com

EUGENE

Bier Stein
345 E. 11th Ave.
541-485-2437
www.thebierstein.com

Sam Bond's Garage
407 Blair Blvd.
541-343-2635
www.sambonds.com

Villard Street Pub
1417 Villard St.
541-393-0960
www.villardstreetpub.com

FLORENCE

Wakonda Brewing
1725 Kingwood St.
541-991-0694

FOREST GROVE

Grand Lodge (hotel)
3505 Pacific Ave.
503-992-9533
www.mcmenamins.com

GEARHART

Sand Trap Bar & Grill
1157 N. Marion Ave.
503-717-8150
www.mcmenamins.com

GOVERNMENT CAMP

**Ice Axe Grill
& Mt. Hood Brewing**
87304 E. Government Camp Loop
503-272-0102
www.iceaxegrill.com

GRANTS PASS

Wild River Pub & Publick House
533 NE E St.
541-474-4456
www.wildriverbrewing.com

GRESHAM

4th Street Brewing
77 NE Fourth St.
503-669-0569
www.4thstreetbrewing.com

HILLSBORO

Helvetia Tavern
10275 NW Helvetia Road
503-647-5286

JOSEPH

Embers Brew House
204 N. Main St.
541-432-2739

Mutiny Brewing
600 N. Main St.
541-432-5274

KLAMATH FALLS

Waldo's Bar & Grill
610 Main St.
541-884-6863
www.checkoutwaldos.com

LA GRANDE

Mt. Emily Ale House
1202 Adams Ave.
541-962-7711
www.mtemilyalehouse.com

LAKE OSWEGO

Gemini Bar & Grill
456 N. State St.
503-636-9445

MANZANITA

Manzanita San Dune Pub
127 Laneda Ave.
503-368-5080
www.sandunepub.com

MCMINNVILLE

Hotel Oregon (hotel)
310 NE Evans St.
503-472-8427
www.mcmenamins.com

MEDFORD

4 Daughters Irish Pub
126 W. Main St.
541-779-4455
www.4daughtersirishpub.com

Kaleidoscope Pizzeria & Pub
3084 Crater Lake Hwy.
541-779-7787
www.kaleidoscopepizza.com

Wild River Brewing & Pizza Co.
2684 N. Pacific Hwy.
541-773-7487
www.wildriverbrewing.com

MOSIER

Thirsty Woman
904 Second Ave.
541-490-2022
www.thirstywoman.com

NEWPORT

Rogue Ales Public House
748 SW Bay Blvd.
541-265-3188
www.rogue.com

OREGON CITY

Highland Stillhouse
201 S. Second St.
503-723-6789
www.highlandstillhouse.com

PACIFIC CITY

Sportsman's Pub-n-Grub
34975 Brooten Rd.
503-965-9991

Twist Tasting Room and Lounge
6425 Pacific Ave.
503-965-6887
www.twistwine.com

PARKDALE

Elliot Glacier Public House
4945 Baseline Dr.
541-352-1022
www.elliotglacierpublichouse.com

PENDLETON

Prodigal Son Brewery
230 SE Court Ave.
541-276-6090
www.prodigalsonbrewery.com

PORTLAND (NORTH)

Hop & Vine
1914 N. Killingsworth St.
503-954-3322
www.thehopandvine.com

Lucky Lab Tap Room
1700 N. Killingsworth St.
503-505-9511
www.luckylab.com

Pix Patisserie (dessert shop)
3901 N. Williams Ave.
503-282-6539
www.pixpatisserie.com

Saraveza Bottle Shop & Pasty Tavern
1004 N. Killingsworth St.
503-206-4252
www.saraveza.com

PORTLAND (NORTHEAST)

Beulahland Coffee & Alehouse
118 NE 28th Ave.
503-235-2794
www.beulahlandpdx.com

Breakside Brewing
820 NE Dekum St.
503-719-6475
www.breaksidebrews.com

Concordia Ale House
3276 NE Killingsworth St.
503-287-3929
www.concordia-ale.com

County Cork Public House
1329 NE Fremont
503-284-4805
www.countycorkpublichouse.com

Kennedy School (hotel)
5736 NE 33rd Ave.
503-249-3983
www.mcmenamins.com

Laurelhurst Theater (cinema)
2735 E. Burnside St.
503-238-4088
www.laurelhursttheater.com

LaurelThirst Public House
2958 NE Glisan St.
503-232-1504
www.laurelthirst.com

Laurelwood PDX
Portland International Airport
7000 NE Airport Way
503-493-9427 (Concourse A)
503-281-6753 (Concourse E)
www.laurelwoodbrewpub.com

Mash Tun Brewpub
2204 NE Alberta St.
503-548-4491
www.themashtunbrewpub.com

Moon & Sixpence
2014 NE 42nd Ave.
503-288-7802

Rogue PDX
Portland International Airport
7000 NE Airport Way
503-282-2630 (Concourse D)
www.rogue.com

Spints Alehouse
401 NE 28th Ave.
503-847-2534
www.spintspdx.com

PORTLAND (NORTHWEST)

Henry's 12th Street Tavern
10 NW 12th Ave.
503-227-5320
www.henrystavern.com

Laurelwood NW Public House
2723 NW Kearney St.
503-228-5553
www.laurelwoodbrewpub.com

Rogue Ales Public House
1339 NW Flanders St.
503-222-5910
www.rogue.com

PORTLAND (SOUTHEAST)

Apex
1216 SE Division St.
503-273-9227
www.apexbar.com

Bagdad Theater (cinema)
3702 SE Hawthorne Blvd.
503-467-7521
www.mcmenamins.com

Bar Avignon
2138 SE Division St.
503-517-0808
www.baravignon.com

Barley Mill
1629 SE Hawthorne Blvd.
503-231-1492
www.mcmenamins.com

Belmont Station & Biercafé
4500 SE Stark St.
503-232-8538
www.belmont-station.com

Blitz Ladd
2239 SE 11th Ave.
503-236-3592
www.blitzbarpdx.net

Blue Monk
3341 SE Belmont St.
503-595-0575
www.thebluemonk.com

Bucket Brigade
8012 SE Powell Blvd.
503-774-8953
www.bucketbrigadesportsbar.com

Cascade Brewing Barrel House
939 SE Belmont St.
503-265-8603
cascadebrewingbarrelhouse.com

Cheese Bar (cheese shop)
6031 SE Belmont St.
503-222-6014
www.cheese-bar.com

Claudia's Sports Pub and Grill
3006 SE Hawthorne Blvd.
503-232-1744
www.claudiaspub.com

Duff's Garage (music hall)
1635 SE Seventh Ave.
503-234-2337
www.duffsgarage.com

EastBurn
1800 E. Burnside St.
503-236-2876
www.theeastburn.com

The Goodfoot (music hall)
2845 SE Stark St.
503-239-9292
www.thegoodfoot.com

Hedge House
3412 SE Division St.
503-235-2215
www.newoldlompoc.com

Horse Brass Pub
4534 SE Belmont St.
503-232-2202
www.horsebrass.com

Morrison Hotel
719 SE Morrison St.
503-236-7080

Muddy Rudder
8105 SE Seventh Ave.
503-233-4410

Oaks Bottom Public House
1612 SE Bybee Blvd.
503-232-1728
www.newoldlompoc.com

Philadelphia's
6410 SE Milwaukie Ave.
503-239-8544
www.phillypdx.com

Pix Patisserie (dessert shop)
3402 SE Division St.
503-232-4407
www.pixpatisserie.com

Produce Row
204 SE Oak St.
503-232-8355
www.producerowcafe.com

Roscoe's
8105 SE Stark St.
503-255-0049

Victory Bar
3652 SE Division St.
503-236-8755
www.thevictorybar.com

PORTLAND (SOUTHWEST)

Bailey's Taproom
213 SW Broadway
503-295-1004
www.baileystaproom.com

Crystal Ballroom (music hall)
1332 W. Burnside St.
503-225-0047
www.mcmenamins.com

Full Sail Brewery at Riverplace
0307 SW Montgomery
503-222-5343
www.fullsailbrewing.com

Higgins
1239 SW Broadway
503-222-9070

Journey's
7771 SW Capitol Hwy.
503-929-0229
www.journeyspdx.com

Lucky Lab Public House
7675 SW Capitol Hwy.
503-244-2537
www.luckylab.com

Old Market Pub & Brewery
6959 SW Multnomah Blvd.
503-244-2337
www.drinkbeerhere.com

**Rock Bottom
Restaurant & Brewery**
206 SW Morrison St.
503-796-2739
www.rockbottom.com

Tugboat Brewing
711 SW Ankeny St.
503-226-2508
www.d2m.com/Tugwebsite

REDMOND

7th Street Brewhouse
855 SW Seventh St.
541-923-1795
www.cascadelakes.com

SALEM

Boon's Treasury
888 Liberty St. NE
503-399-9062
www.mcmenamins.com

f/stop Fitzgerald's Public House
335 Grove St. NE
www.f-stoppub.com

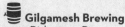 **The Ram**
515 12th St.
503-363-1905
www.theram.com

Thompson Brewery & Public House
3575 Liberty Rd. S.
503-363-7286
www.mcmenamins.com

SEASIDE

Harbor Bite
220 Ave. U
503-738-7444

SILVERTON

Seven Brides Brewing
990 N, First St.
503-874-4677
www.sevenbridesbrewing.com

SISTERS

Three Creeks Brewing
721 Desperado Court
541-549-1963
www.threecreeksbrewing.com

THE DALLES

Clock Tower Ales
311 Union St.
541-705-3590
www.clocktowerales.com

TIGARD

Fanno Creek Brewpub
12562 SW Main St.
503-624-9400
www.fannocreekbrewpub.com

TURNER

 **Gilgamesh Brewing**
2953 Ridgeway Dr.
503-779-9686
www.gilgameshbrewing.com

WEST LINN

Philadelphia's
18625 Hwy. 43
503-699-4130
www.phillypdx.com

 **WASHINGTON**

ANACORTES

Brown Lantern Ale House
412 Commercial Ave.
360-293-2544
www.brownlantern.com

BATTLE GROUND

Laurelwood Public House
1401 SE Rasmussen Blvd.
360-723-0937
www.laurelwoodbrewpub.com

BELLINGHAM

Archer Alehouse
1212 Tenth St.
360-647-7002
www.thearcheralehouse.com

Copper Hog Gastropub
1327 N. State St.
360-927-7888
www.thecopperhog.com

Green Frog Café Acoustic Tavern
902 N. State St.
360-756-1213
www.acoustictavern.com

McKay's Taphouse/Pizza Pipeline
1118 E. Maple St.
360-647-3600

Uisce Irish Pub
1319 Commercial St.
360-738-7939
uisceirishpub.com

BUCKLEY

Elk Head Brewing
28120 State Route 410 E
360-829-2739

CAMANO ISLAND

Camano Lodge
Diamond Knot Brewing Co.
170 Cross Island Rd.
360-387-9972
www.diamondknot.com

CONCRETE

Birdsview Brewing
38302 State Route 20
360-826-3406
www.birdsviewbrewingco.com

DAYTON

Skye Book & Brew
148 E. Main St.
509-382-4677
www.skyebookandbrew.com

ELLENSBURG

Iron Horse Brewing
1000 Prospect St.
509-933-3134
www.ironhorsebrewery.com

GIG HARBOR

7 Seas Brewing
3207 57th St. Ct. NW
253-514-8129
www.7seasbrewing.com

KENNEWICK

The Marina
Ice Harbor Brewing Co.
350 Clover Island Dr.
509-586-3181
www.iceharbor.com

KINGSTON

Hood Canal Brewery
26499 Bond Rd. NE
360-297-8316
www.hoodcanalbrewery.com

LA CONNER

La Conner Brewing
117 S. First St.
360-466-1415
www.laconnerbrew.com

LYNNWOOD

Ellersick Brewing
5030 208th St. SW
425-672-7051
www.ellersickbrewing.com

MILTON

Milton Tavern
7320 Pacific Hwy. E.
253-922-3340
www.themiltontavern.com

MOUNT VERNON

Porterhouse Pub
416 Gates
360-336-9989
www.porterhousepub.net

Skagit River Brewery
404 S. Third St.
360-336-2884
www.skagitbrew.com

NORTHPORT

Northern Ales
118 Center Ave.
509-732-6200
www.northernales.com

OAK HARBOR

Flyers Restaurant & Brewery
32295 State Route 20
360-675-5858
www.eatatflyers.com

OLYMPIA

Eastside Club Tavern
410 Fourth Ave. E.
360-357-9985
www.theeastsideclub.com

4th Avenue Ale House
210 Fourth Ave. E.
360-786-1444
www.the4thave.com

OROVILLE

Alpine Brewing
821 14th Ave.
509-476-9662
www.alpine-brewing.com

POULSBO

Valhöll Brewing
20186 B Front St. NE
360-990-3899
www.valhollbrewing.com

PROSSER

Horse Heaven Hills Brewery
1118 Meade Ave.
509-781-6400
horseheavenhillsbrewery.food.officelive.com

Whitstran Brewing
1427 Wine Country Rd.
509-786-4922
www.whitstranbrewing.com

PUYALLUP

Powerhouse
454 East Main
253-845-1370
www.powerhousebrewpub.com

REDMOND

Black Raven Brewing
14679 NE 95th St.
425-881-3020
www.blackravenbrewing.com

Malt & Vine
16851 Redmond Way
425-881-6461
www.maltandvine.com

RENTON

Dog & Pony Alehouse and Grill
351 Park Ave. N.
425-254-8080
www.thedogandpony.com

Whistle Stop Ale House
809 S. Fourth St.
425-277-3039
www.whistlestopalehouse.com

RICHLAND

Atomic Ale
1015 Lee Blvd.
509-946-5465
www.atomicalebrewpub.com

ROSLYN

Roslyn Brewing
208 Pennsylvania Ave.
509-649-2232
www.roslynbrewery.com

SEATTLE (CAPITOL HILL)

Barca
1510 11th Ave.
206-325-8263
www.barcaseattle.com

Feierabend
422 Yale Ave. N.
206-340-2528
www.feierabendseattle.com

Hopvine
507 15th Ave. E.
206-328-3120
www.3pubs.com

Linda's Tavern
707 E. Pine St.
206-325-1220
www.lindastavern.com

Quinn's
1001 E. Pike St.
206-325-7711
www.quinnspubseattle.com

Smith Pub
332 15th Ave. E.
206-709-1900
www.smithpub.com

Stumbling Monk
1635 E. Olive Way
206-860-0916

Summit Public House
601 Summit Ave. E.
206-324-7611
www.summitpublichouse.com

SEATTLE (DOWNTOWN)

Collins Pub
526 Second Ave.
206-623-1016
www.thecollinspub.com

Epic Ales
3201 First Ave. S.
206-351-3637
www.epicales.com

Tap House Grill
1506 Sixth Ave.
206-816-3314
www.taphousegrill.com

Two Bells
2313 Fourth Ave.
206-441-3050
www.thetwobells.com

Virginia Inn
1937 First Ave.
206-728-1937
www.virginiainnseattle.com

White Horse Trading Company
1908 Post Alley
206-441-7767

SEATTLE (FREMONT–BALLARD)

Barking Dog Alehouse
705 NW 70th St.
206-782-2974
www.thebarkingdogalehouse.com

Brouwer's Café
400 N. 35th St.
206-267-2437
www.brouwerscafe.blogspot.com

The Dray
708 NW 65th St.
206-453-4527
www.thedray.com

Old Pequliar
1722 NW Market St.
206-782-8886

Old Town Ale House
5233 Ballard Ave. NW
206-782-8323
www.oldtownalehouse.com

Park Pub
6114 Phinney Ave. N.
206-789-8187
www.theparkpub.com

People's Pub
5429 Ballard Ave. NW
206-783-6521
www.peoplespub.com

Reading Gaol
418 NW 65th St.
206-783-3002
www.readinggaol.com

Red Door
3401 Evanston Ave. N.
206-547-7521
www.reddoorseattle.com

Sully's Snowgoose Saloon
6119 Phinney Ave. N.
206-782-9231

SEATTLE (GREEN LAKE–WALLINGFORD–PHINNEY RIDGE)

Duck Island Ale House
7317 Aurora Ave. N.
206-783-3360

Fremont Brewing
3409 Woodland Park Ave. N.
206-420-2407
www.fremontbrewing.com

Latona Pub
6423 Latona Ave. NE
206-525-2238
www.3pubs.com

Tangletown
Elysian Brewing Co.
2106 N. 55th St.
206-547-5929
www.elysianbrewing.com

Über Tavern
7517 Aurora Ave. N.
206-782-2337
www.uberbier.com

SEATTLE (GREENWOOD–BROADVIEW)

Pillager's Pub
8551 Greenwood Ave. N.
206-706-2779
ww.pillagerspub.com

Prost! Tavern
7311 Greenwood Ave. N.
206-706-5430
www.prosttavern.net

Pub at Piper's Creek
10527 Greenwood Ave. N.
206-417-5734

74th Street Ale House
7401 Greenwood Ave. N.
206-784-2955
www.seattlealehouses.com/74th/beer.asp

SEATTLE (LAKE CITY—WEDGWOOD—RAVENNA)

Cooper's Alehouse
8065 Lake City Way NE
206-522-2923
www.coopersalehouse.com

Die BierStube
6106 Roosevelt Way NE
206-527-7019
www.diebierstube.com

Fiddler's Inn
9219 35th Ave. NE
206-525-0752
www.3pubs.com

Hudson New American Public House
8014 15th Ave. NE
206-524-5070
www.hudsonpublichouse.com

Pies and Pints
1215 NE 65th St.
206-524-7082
www.piesandpints.com

The Pub at Third Place
6504 20th Ave. NE
206-523-0217
www.vioscafe.com/viospub.html

Wedgwood Ale House & Café
8515 35th Ave. NE
206-527-2676
www.wedgwoodalehouse.com

SEATTLE (SOUTH)

Hooverville
1721 First Ave. S.
206-264-2428
www.hoovervilleseattle.com

9 lb. Hammer
6009 Airport Way S.
206-762-3373
www.ninepoundhammer.com

Two Beers Brewing
4700 Ohio Ave. S.
206-762-0490
www.twobeersbrewery.com

SEATTLE (UNIVERSITY DISTRICT)

College Inn Pub
4006 University Way NE
206-634-2307

Montlake Ale House
2307 24th Ave. E.
206-726-5968
www.montlakealehouse.net

Northlake Tavern and Pizza House
660 NE Northlake Way
206-633-5317
www.northlaketavern.com

Shultzy's Sausage
4114 University Way NE
206-548-9461
www.shultzys.com

SEATTLE (WEST)

Beveridge Place Pub
6413 California Ave. SW
206-932-9906
www.beveridgeplacepub.com

Porterhouse
2329 California Ave. SW
206-932-2575
www.westcoastales.com/ph.seattle

Prost! West Seattle
3047 California Ave. SW
206-420-7174
www.prosttavern.net

SNOQUALMIE

Snoqualmie Brewery
8032 Falls Ave. SE
425-831-2357
www.fallsbrew.com

SPOKANE

Baby Bar
827 W. First Ave.
509-847-1234

Blue Spark
15 S. Howard St.
509-838-5787
www.bluesparkspokane.com

Elk Public House
1931 W. Pacific Ave.
509-363-1973
www.wedonthaveone.com

Far West Billiards (pool hall)
1001 W. First Ave.
509-455-3429
www.farwestbilliards.com

Post Street Ale House (hotel)
Hotel Lusso
1 N. Post St.
509-789-6900
www.hotellusso.com

Swamp Tavern
1904 W. Fifth Ave.
509-458-2337

Viking Tavern
1221 N. Stevens St.
509-326-2942

TACOMA

The Hub
203 Tacoma Ave. S.
253-683-4606
www.hub.harmonbrewingco.com

Parkway Tavern
313 N. I St.
253-383-8748

Red Hot
2914 Sixth Ave.
253-779-0229
www.redhottacoma.com

The Spar
2121 N. 30th St.
253-627-8215
www.the-spar.com

The Swiss
1904 Jefferson Ave.
253-572-2821
www.theswisspub.com

TWISP

Twisp River Pub
Methow Valley Brewing Co.
201 Highway 20
888-220-3360
www.methowbrewing.com

VANCOUVER

Salmon Creek Brewery and Pub
108 W. Evergreen Blvd.
360-993-1827
www.salmoncreekbrewpub.com

WAITSBURG

Whetstone Public House
110 Preston Ave.
509-337-6088

WALLA WALLA

Mill Creek Brewing
11 S. Palouse
509-522-2440
www.millcreek-brewpub.com

YAKIMA

Yakima Craft Brewing
2920 River Rd.
509-654-7357
www.yakimacraftbrewing.com

BRITISH COLUMBIA

FIELD

Cathedral Mountain Lodge (hotel)
1 Yoho Valley Rd.
866-619-6442
www.cathedralmountain.com

KELOWNA

Doc Willoughby's Downtown Pub
353 Bernard Ave.
250-868-8288
www.docwilloughby.com

**Freddy's Brew Pub/
McCurdy's Bowl (bowling alley)**
Mill Creek Brewery
948 McCurdy Rd.
250-491-2695
www.mccurdybowl.com

NELSON

Nelson Brewing
512 Latimer St.
250-352-3582
www.nelsonbrewing.com

NORTH VANCOUVER

Sailor Hagar's Brew Pub
86 Semisch Ave.
604-984-3087
www.bestbeerbc.com

OSOYOOS

Ridge Brew House
9907 Hwy. 3
250-495-7679
www.westridgeinn.com/restaurant.asp

PEACHLAND

Gasthaus on the Lake
5790 Beach Ave.
250-767-6625
www.gasthaus.ca

PENTICTON

Barley Mill
2460 Skaha Lake Rd.
250-493-8000
www.barleymillpub.com

Kettle Valley Station
1070 Eckhardt Ave. W.
250-493-3388
www.kettlevalleystation.com

RICHMOND

Flying Beaver
4760 Inglis Dr.
604-273-0278
www.markjamesgroup.com

SUMMERLAND

Local Lounge and Grille
12817 Lakeshore Dr. S.
250-494-8855

SURREY

Big Ridge
5580 152nd St.
604-574-2739
www.markjamesgroup.com

VANCOUVER

Alibi Room
157 Alexander St.
604-623-3383
www.alibi.ca

Chambar
562 Beatty St.
604-879-7119
www.chambar.com

**Dockside Restaurant
& Brewery**
1253 Johnston St.
604-685-7070
www.docksidevancouver.com

Granville Island Brewing
1441 Cartwright St.
604-687-2739
www.gib.ca

Irish Heather
210 Carrall St.
604-688-9779
www.irishheather.com

Railway Club
579 Dunsmuir St.
604-681-1625
www.railwayclub.com

Whip Restaurant & Gallery
209 E. Sixth Ave.
604-874-4687
www.thewhiprestaurant.com

VICTORIA

Christie's Carriage House
1739 Fort St.
250-598-5333
www.christiespub.com

Garrick's Head Pub
69 Bastion Square
250-384-6835
www.bedfordregency.com/pub.htm

Local Kitchen
1205 Wharf St.
250-385-1999
www.thelocalkitchen.ca

Six Mile Pub
494 Island Hwy
250-478-3121
www.sixmilepub.com

Sticky Wicket Pub
919 Douglas St.
250-383-7137
www.strathconahotel.com/the_sticky_wicket_
pub__restau.html

WEST KELOWNA

13 Monks Taphouse & Grill
2569 Dobbin Rd.
250-707-3644
www.13monks.com

BEST BOTTLE SHOPS

 **OREGON**

Bear Creek Beers
410 E. Main St.
Medford
541-773-7564
www.bearcreekbeers.com

The Beermongers
1125 SE Division St.
Portland
503-234-6012
www.thebeermongers.com

Belmont Station & Biercafé
4500 SE Stark St.
Portland
503-232-8538
www.belmont-station.com

Bier One
424 SW Coast Hwy.
Newport
541-265-4630
www.bier-one.com

Bier Stein
345 E. 11th Ave.
Eugene
541-485-2437
www.thebierstein.com

Birra Deli
18749 SW Martinazzi Ave.
Tualatin
503-783-1037
www.birradeli.com

The Bobolink
1102 Washington Ave.
La Grande
541-963-2888

Brew Shop
2524 NE Division St.
Bend
541-323-2318
www.homesuds.com

Concordia Ale House
3276 NE Killingsworth St.
Portland
503-287-3929
www.concordia-ale.com

John's Market
3535 SW Multnomah Blvd.
Portland
503-244-2617
www.johnsmarketplace.com

Portland Street Market
1842 Portland St.
Klamath Falls
541-884-0010
www.facebook.com/portlandstreetmarket

Saraveza Bottle Shop & Pasty Tavern
1004 N. Killingsworth St.
Portland
503-206-4252
www.saraveza.com

Wine Haus
1111 N. Roosevelt Dr.
Seaside
503-738-0201

Woodstock Wine & Deli
4030 SE Woodstock Blvd.
Portland
503-777-2208
www.woodstockwineanddeli.com

 **WASHINGTON**

Beer Authority
12716 Lake City Way NE
Seattle
206-417-9629
www.seattlebeerauthority.com

Big Star Beers
1117 N. Northgate Way
Seattle
206-729-0797
www.bigstarbeers.com

Bottleworks
1710 N. 45th St.
Seattle
206-633-2437
www.bottleworks.com

By the Bottle
104 W. Evergreen Blvd.
Vancouver
360-696-0012
www.bottledbrews.com

Full Throttle Bottles
5909 Airport Way S.
Seattle
206-763-2079
www.fullthrottlebottles.com

Gravity Beer Market
1001 Fourth Ave. E.
Olympia
360-352-5107
www.gravitybeermarket.com

99 Bottles
35002 Pacific Hwy. S.
Federal Way
253-838-2558
www.99bottles.net

Pike Street Beer & Wine
518 E. Pike St.
Seattle
206-778-1086
www.pikestreetbeer.com

Red House
410 Burnett Ave. S.
Renton
425-226-2666
www.redhousebeerandwine.com

West Richland Beer & Wine
4033 W. Van Giesen
West Richland
509-967-9726

Whidbey Beer Works
710 SE Fidalgo Ave.
Oak Harbor
360-675-8570
www.whidbeybeerworks.com

BRITISH COLUMBIA

Avalon Cold Beer & Wine
1025 Marine Dr.
North Vancouver
604-984-6985

Brewery Creek Cold Beer & Wine
3045 Main St.
Vancouver
604-872-3373
www.brewerycreekliquorstore.com

Firefly Fine Wines & Ales
2857 Cambie St.
Vancouver
604-875-3325
www.fireflyfinewinesandales.com

Sailor Hagar's Liquor Store
211 W. First St.
North Vancouver
604-984-2337
www.bestbeerbc.com

Spinnakers
425 Simcoe St. / 130-176 Wilson St.
Victoria, 250-590-3515 / 250-360-1333
www.spiritmerchants.ca

INDEX

Colin Westcott

LISA MORRISON is host and producer of *Beer O'Clock!*, the Pacific Northwest's only weekly, hour-long commercial radio show devoted to craft beer. She writes for nearly every beer-related magazine in the country and has been teaching beer-tasting classes in and around Portland, Oregon, for more than a decade. Visit her at www.thebeergoddess.com.